CLASSIC SERMONS
ON
THE SOVEREIGNTY OF GOD

CLASSIC SERMONS

ON

THE SOVEREIGNTY OF GOD

Compiled by
Warren W. Wiersbe

HENDRICKSON
PUBLISHERS

Classic Sermons on the Sovereignty of God
Hendrickson Publishers, Inc. edition
ISBN 1-56563-156-0

This edition is published by special arrangement with
and permission of Kregel Publications. Copyright © 1994
by Kregel Publications, a division of Kregel, Inc. P.O. Box
2607, Grand Rapids, MI 49501.

Printed in the United States of America

CONTENTS

5

LIST OF SCRIPTURE TEXTS

PREFACE

THE KREGEL CLASSIC SERMONS SERIES is an attempt to assemble and publish meaningful sermons from master preachers about significant themes.

These are *sermons*, not essays or chapters taken from books about themes. Not all of these sermons could be called "great," but all of them are *meaningful*. They apply the truths of the Bible to the needs of the human heart which is something that all effective preaching must do.

While some are better known than others, all of the preachers, whose sermons I have selected, had important ministries and were highly respected in their day. The fact that a sermon is included in this volume does not mean that either the compiler or the publisher agrees with or endorses everything that the man did, preached, or wrote. The sermon is here because it has a valued contribution to make.

These are sermons about *significant* themes. The pulpit is no place to play with trivia. The preacher has thirty minutes in which to help mend broken hearts, change defeated lives, and save lost souls; one can never accomplish this demanding ministry by distributing homiletical tidbits. In these difficult days, we do not need "clever" pulpiteers who discuss the times; we need dedicated ambassadors who will preach the eternities.

The reading of these sermons can enrich your own spiritual life. The studying of them can enrich your own skills as an interpreter and expounder of God's truth. However God uses these sermons in your own life and ministry, my prayer is that His church around the world will be encouraged and strengthened.

WARREN W. WIERSBE

The Government of God Desirable

Lyman Beecher (1775–1863) was born in New Haven, Connecticut, in 1775. He graduated from Yale in 1797 and in 1798 took charge of the Presbyterian Church at Easthampton, Long Island. He first attracted attention by his sermon on the death of Alexander Hamilton and in 1810 became pastor of the Congregational Church at Litchfield, Connecticut. In the course of a pastorate of 16 years, he preached a remarkable series of sermons on temperance and became recognized as one of the foremost pulpit orators of the country. In 1826 he went to Boston as pastor of the Hanover Street Congregational Church. Six years later he became president of the Lane Theological Seminary in Ohio, an office he retained for twenty years. In 1852 he returned to Boston and subsequently retired to the house of his son, Henry Ward Beecher, where he died in 1863.

This sermon is taken from *Treasury of the World's Great Sermons*, edited by Warren W. Wiersbe and published by Kregel Publications.

Lyman Beecher

1

THE GOVERNMENT OF GOD DESIRABLE

Thy will be done in earth as it is in heaven (Matthew 6:10).

IN THIS passage we are instructed to pray that the world may be governed and not abandoned to the miseries of unrestrained sin; that God Himself would govern and not another; and that God would administer the government of the world, in all respects, according to His own pleasure. The passage is a formal surrender to God of power and dominion over the earth as entire as His dominion is in His heaven. The petition, therefore, "Thy will be done," contains the doctrine:

> That it is greatly to be desired that God should govern the world, and dispose of men, in all respects, entirely according to His own pleasure.

The truth of this doctrine is so manifest that it would seem to rank itself in the number of self-evident propositions, incapable of proof clearer than its own light, had not experience taught that, of all truths, it is the most universally and bitterly controverted. Plain as it is, it has occasioned more argument than any other doctrine; and, by argument merely, it has gained fewer proselytes. For it is one of those controversies in which the heart decides wholly, and argument, strong or feeble, is alike ineffectual.

This consideration would present, on the threshold, a hopeless impediment to further progress did we not know, also, that arguments a thousand times repeated, and as often resisted, may at length become mighty through God to the casting down of imaginations and every high thing that exalts itself against the knowledge of God. I shall, therefore, suggest several considerations to confirm this most obvious truth that it is desirable that God should govern the world entirely according to His own good pleasure.

God Knows Best

It is desirable that God should govern the world and dispose of all events according to His pleasure because He knows perfectly in what manner it is best that the world should be governed.

The best way of disposing of men and their concerns is that which will effectually illustrate the glory of God. The glory of God is His benevolence, and His natural attributes for the manifestation of it, and sun of the moral universe, the light and life of His kingdom. All the blessedness of the intelligent creation arises, and ever will arise, from the manifestation and apprehension of the glory of God. It was to manifest this glory that the worlds were created. It was that there might be creatures to behold and enjoy God, that His dominions were peopled with intelligent beings. And it is that His holy subjects may see and enjoy Him, that He upholds and governs the universe. The entire importance of our world, therefore, and of men and their concerns, is relative and is great or small only as we are made to illustrate the glory of God. How this important end shall be most effectually accomplished none but Himself is able to determine. He, only, knows how so to order things as that the existence of every being, and every event, shall answer the purpose of its creation. From the rolling of a world to the fall of a sparrow shall conspire to increase the exhibitions of the divine character and expand the joy of the holy universe.

An inferior intelligence at the helm of government might conceive very desirable purposes of benevolence and still be at a loss as to the means most fit and effectual to accomplish them. But with God there is no such deficiency. In Him the knowledge which discovered the end discovers also, with unerring wisdom, the most appropriate means to bring it to pass. He is wise in heart; He has established the world by His wisdom and stretched out the heavens by His discretion. And is He not wise enough to be intrusted with the government of the world? Who, then, shall be His counselor? Who shall supply the deficiencies of His skill? Oh, the presumption of vain man! And, oh! the depths both of the wisdom and knowledge of God!

God Is Able

It is desirable that God should govern the world according to His own pleasure, because He is entirely able to execute His purposes.

A wise politician perceives, often, both the end and the means and is still unable to bring to pass his counsels because the means, though wise, are beyond his control. But God is as able to execute as He is to plan. Having chosen the end, and selected the means, his counsels stand. He is the Lord God omnipotent. The whole universe is a storehouse of means; and when He speaks, every intelligence and every atom flies to execute His pleasure. The omnipotence of God in giving efficacy to His government inspires and perpetuates the ecstasy of heaven. "And a voice came out from the throne, saying, Praise our God. And I heard as it were the voice of a great multitude, and as the voice of many waters, and as the voice of many thunderings, saying Alleluia, the Lord God omnipotent reigneth." What will that man do in heaven who is afraid and reluctant to commit to God the government of the earth? And what will become of those who, unable to frustrate His counsels, murmur and rebel against His providence?

God Is Always Good

It is desirable that God should govern the world according to His pleasure because the pleasure of God is always good.

The angels who kept not their first estate, and many wicked men, have great knowledge, and skill, and power. And yet, on these accounts, are only the more terrible because they employ these mighty faculties to do evil. And the government of God, were He a being of malevolence, armed as He is with skill and power, would justly fill the universe with dismay. But, as it is, brethren, "let not your hearts be troubled." With God there is no perversion of attributes. He is as good as He is wise and powerful. God is love! Love is that glory of God which He has undertaken to express to His intelligent creation in His works. The sole object of the government of God, from beginning to end, is to express His benevolence. His eternal decrees, of which so many are afraid, are nothing but the plan which God has devised to express His benevolence and to make His kingdom as vast and as blest as His own infinite goodness desires. It was to show His glory—to express, in action, His benevolence—that He created all the worlds that roll and rejoice and speak His name through the regions of space. It is to accomplish the same blest design that He upholds and places under law every intelligent being and directs every event, causing every movement in every world to fall in, in its appointed time and place and to unite in promoting the grand result—the glory of God and the highest good of His kingdom. And is there a mortal who, from this great system of blest government, would wish this earth to be an exception? What sort of beings must those be who are afraid of a government administered by infinite benevolence to express, so far as it can be expressed, the infinite goodness of God? I repeat the question—What kind of characters must those be who feel as if they had good reason to fear a government the sole object of which is to express the immeasurable goodness of God?

God Desires to Govern

It is greatly to be desired that God should govern the world according to His pleasure because it is His pleasure to rule as a moral governor.

A moral government is a government exercised over free agents—accountable beings; a government of laws, administered by motives.

The importance of such a government below is manifest from the consideration that it is in His moral government, chiefly, that the glory of God is displayed.

The superintendence of an empty world, or a world of mere animals, would not exhibit at all the moral character of God. The glory of God, shining in His law, could never be made manifest; the brighter glory of God, as displayed in the gospel, must remain forever hid. All that happiness of which we are capable as moral beings, the joys of religion below and the boundless joys of heaven above, would be extinguished in a moment by the suspension of the divine moral government.

Will any pretend that the Almighty cannot maintain a moral government on earth if He governs according to His own pleasure? Can He wield the elements and control at His pleasure every work of His hands but just the mind of man? Is the most noble work of God—that which is the most worthy of attention, and in reference to which all beside is upheld and governed—itself wholly unmanageable? Has Omnipotence formed minds which, the moment they are made, escape from His hands and defy the control of their Maker? Has the Almighty erected a moral kingdom which He cannot govern without destroying its moral nature? Can He only watch and mend and rectify the lawless wanderings of mind? Has He filled the earth with untamed and untamable spirits whose wickedness and rebellion He can merely mitigate but cannot control? Does He superintend a world of madmen full of darkness and disorder cheered and blest by no internal pervading government of His own? Are we bound to submit to all events as parts of the holy providence of God; and yet, is there actually no hand of God controlling the movements of the moral world?

But if the Almighty can, and if He does, govern the earth as a part of His moral kingdom, is there any method of government more safe and wise than that which pleases God? Can there be a better government? We may safely pray, then, "Thy will be done in earth as it is in heaven," without fearing at all the loss of moral agency. For all the glory of God, in His Law and Gospel, and all the eternal manifestations of glory to principalities and powers in heavenly places, depend wholly upon the fact that men, though living under the government of God and controlled according to His pleasure, are still entirely free and accountable for all the deeds done in the body.

There could be no justice in punishment and no condescension, no wisdom, no mercy, in the glorious gospel did not the government of God, though administered according to His pleasure, include and insure the accountable agency of man.

Seeing, therefore, that all the glory of God, which He ever proposes to manifest to the intelligent creation, is to be made known by the Church, is to shine in the face of Jesus Christ, and is to depend upon the perfect consistency of the moral government of God with human freedom, we have boundless assurance that among His absolute, immutable, eternal purposes one, and a leading one, is so to govern the world according to His counsels that, if men sin, there shall be complete desert of punishment and boundless mercy in their redemption.

God Governs in Mercy

It is greatly to be desired that God should rule in the earth according to His pleasure because it is His pleasure to govern the world in mercy by Jesus Christ.

The government is in the hand of a Mediator by whom God is reconciling the world to Himself, not imputing their trespasses to them that believe. Mercy is the bestowment of pardon upon the sinful and undeserving. Now, mankind is so eminently sinful that no government but one administered in infinite mercy could afford the least consolation. Had any being but the God of mercy lit upon the throne, or any will but His will prevailed, there would have been no plan of redemption and no purposes of election to perplex and alarm the wicked. There would have been but one decree and that would have been destruction to the whole race of man.

Are any reluctant to be entirely in the hands of God? Are they afraid to trust Him to dispose of soul and body for time and eternity? Let them surrender their mercies then and go out naked from that government which feeds, protects and comforts them. Let them give up their Bibles, relinquish the means of grace and the hopes of glory, and descend and make their bed in hell, where they have long since deserved to be and where they long since would have been, if God had not governed the world according to His own good pleasure. If they would escape the evils which they fear from the hand of God, let them abandon the blessings they receive from it. They will soon discover whether the absolute dominion of God and their dependence upon Him be, in reality, a ground of murmuring and alarm. Our only hope of heaven arises from being entirely in the hands of God. Our destruction could not be made more certain than it would be were we to be given up to our own disposal or to the disposal of any being but God. Would sinful mortals change their own hearts? Could the combined universe, without God, change the depraved affections of men? Surely, then, we have cause for unceasing joy that we are in the hands of God, seeing He is a God of mercy and has decreed to rule in mercy, and actually is administering the government of the world in mercy, by Jesus Christ.

We have nothing to fear from the entire dominion of God which we should not have cause equally to fear as outcasts from the divine government. But we have everything to hope while He rules the earth according to His most merciful pleasure. The Lord reigns; let the earth rejoice, let the multitude of the isles be glad. It is of the Lord's mercies that we are not consumed because His compassions fail not.

God Governs in Justice

It is greatly to be desired that God should dispose of mankind according to His pleasure because, if He does so, it is certain that there will be no injustice done to anyone.

He will do no injustice to His holy kingdom by any whom He saves. He will bring none to heaven who are not holy and prepared for heaven. He will bring none there in any way not consistent with His perfections and the best good of His kingdom; none in any way but that prescribed in the gospel, the way of faith in Jesus Christ, of repentance for sin, and of good works as the constituted fruit and evidence of faith.

Earthly monarchs have their favorites whom, if guilty of a violation of the laws, they will often interpose to save, although the welfare of the kingdom requires their punishment. But God has no such favorites—He is no respecter of persons. He spared not the angels; upon the earth distinctions of intellect, or wealth, or honor will have no effect. He only that believes shall be saved. The great and the learned shall not be obtruded upon heaven without holiness because they are great or learned; the humble and contrite shall not be excluded because they are poor, ignorant, or obscure. God has provided a way for all men to return to Him. He has opened the door of their prison and set open before them a door of admission into the kingdom of His dear Son. He commanded and entreated them to abandon their dreary abode and come into the glorious liberty of the sons of God. But all, with one consent, refuse to comply. Each prefers his own loathsome dwelling to the building of God and chooses, steadfastly, the darkness of his own dungeon to the light of God's kingdom.

But, as God has determined that the redemption of His Son shall not be unavailing through human obstinacy, so He has chosen, in Christ, multitudes which no man can number that they should be holy and without blame before Him in love. And in bringing these sons and daughters to glory through sanctification of the Spirit and belief of the truth, He will introduce not one whom all the inhabitants of heaven will not hail joyfully as the companion of their glory. And if God does in the earth just as He pleases, He will make willing and obedient and bring to heaven just those persons who it was most desirable should come. And He will bring just as many obstinate rebels to abandon their prison and enter cheerfully His kingdom as infinite wisdom, goodness, and mercy see fit and desire. He will not mar His glory or the happiness of His kingdom, by bringing in too many nor by omitting to bring in enough. His redeemed kingdom, as to the number and the persons who compose it and the happiness included in it, will be such as shall be wholly satisfactory to God and to every subject of His kingdom.

And if God governs according to His pleasure, He will do no injustice to His impenitent enemies. He will send to misery no harmless animals without souls—no mere machines—none who have done, or even attempted to do, as well as they could. He will leave to walk in their own way none who do not deserve to be left; He will punish none for walking in it who did not walk therein knowingly, deliberately and with willful obstinacy. He will give up to death none who did not choose death and choose it with as entire freedom as Himself chooses holiness and who did not deserve eternal punishment as truly as Himself deserves eternal praise. He will send to hell none who are not opposed to Him, to holiness, and to heaven; none who are not, by voluntary sin and rebellion, unfitted for heaven and fitted for destruction as eminently as saints are prepared for glory. He will consign to perdition no poor, feeble, inoffensive beings, sacrificing one innocent creature to increase the happiness of another. He will cause the punishment of the wicked to illustrate His glory, and thus indirectly to promote the happiness of heaven. But God will not illumine heaven with His glory and fill it with praise by sacrificing helpless, unoffending creatures to eternal torment; nor will He doom to hell one whom He will not convince also that he deserves to go thither. The justice of God, in the condemnation of the impenitent, will be as unquestionable as His infinite mercy will be in the salvation of the redeemed.

If the will of God is done on earth among men, there will be no more injustice done to the inhabitants of the earth than there is done to the blessed in heaven. Was it ever known—did any ever complain—was it ever conceived—that God was a tyrant in heaven? Why, then, should we question the justice of His government on earth? Is He not the same God below as above? Are not all His attributes equally employed? Does He not govern for the same end, and will not His government below conspire to promote the same joyful end as His government above?

God Governs by His Own Counsel

It is greatly to be desired that God should govern the world according to His pleasure because His own infinite blessedness, as well as the happiness of His kingdom, depends upon His working all things according to the counsel of His own will.

Could the Almighty be prevented from expressing the benevolence of His nature, according to His purposes, His present boundless blessedness would become the pain of ungratified desire. God is love, and His happiness consists in the exercise and expression of it, according to His own eternal purpose which He purposed in Christ Jesus before the world began. It is therefore declared, "The Lord hath made all things for himself"; that is, to express and gratify His infinite benevolence. The moral excellence of God does not consist in quiescent love but in love active, bursting forth and abounding. Nor does the divine happiness arise from the contemplation of idle perfections, but from perfections which comprehend boundless capacity and activity in doing good.

From what has been said, we may be led to contemplate with satisfaction the infinite blessedness of God.

God is love! This is a disposition which, beyond all others, is happy in its own nature. He is perfect in love; there is, therefore, in His happiness no alloy. His love is infinite and, of course, His blessedness is unbounded. If the little holiness existing in good men, though balanced by remaining sin, occasions at times unutterable joy, how blessed must God be who is perfectly and infinitely holy! It is to be remembered, also, that the benevolence of God is at all times perfectly gratified. The universe which God has created and upholds, including what He has done and what He will yet do, will be brought into a condition which will satisfy His infinite benevolence. The great plan of government which God has chosen and which His power and wisdom will execute, will embrace as much good as in the nature of things is possible. He is not, like erring man, straitened and perplexed through lack of knowledge or power. There is in His plan no defect and in His execution no failure. God, therefore, is infinitely happy in His holiness and in the expression of it which it pleases Him to make.

The revolt of angels, the fall of man, and the miseries of sin do not for a moment interrupt the blessedness of God. They were not to Him unexpected events, starting up suddenly while the watchman of Israel slumbered. They were foreseen by God as clearly as any other events of His government and have occasioned neither perplexity nor dismay. With infinite complacency He beholds still His unshaken counsels and with almighty hand rolls on His undisturbed decrees. Surrounded by unnumbered millions created by His hand and upheld by His power, He shines forth—God over all, blest forever. What an object of joyful contemplation then is the blessedness of God! It is infinite; His boundless capacity is full. It is eternal; He is God blest forever. The happiness of the created universe is but a drop—a drop to the mighty ocean of divine enjoyment. How delightful the thought that in God there is such an immensity of joy beyond the reach of vicissitude! When we look around below, a melancholy sensation pervades the mind. What miserable creatures! What a wretched world! But when, from this scene of darkness and misery, we look up to the throne of God and behold Him high above the darkness and miseries of sin, dwelling in light inaccessible and full of glory, the prospect brightens. If a few rebels who refuse to love and participate in His munificence are groping in darkness on His footstool, God is light and in Him there is no darkness at all.

Those who are opposed to the decrees of God and to His sovereignty, as displayed in the salvation of sinners, are enemies of God.

They are unwilling that His will should be done in earth as it is in heaven; the decrees of God are nothing but His choice as to the manner in which He will govern His own kingdom. He did not enter upon His government to learn wisdom by experience. Before they were yet formed, His vast dominion lay open to His view; before He took the reins of created empire, He saw in what manner it became Him to govern. His ways are everlasting. Known unto God are all His works from the beginning. To be opposed to the decrees of God, therefore, is to be unwilling that God should have any choice concerning the government of the world. And can those be willing that God should govern the world entirely according to His pleasure who object to His having any pleasure upon the subject? To object to the choice of God, with respect to the management of the world and because it is eternal, is to object to the existence of God. A God of eternal knowledge without an eternal will or choice would be a God without moral character.

To suppose that God did not know what events would exist in His kingdom is to divest Him of omniscience. To suppose that He did know and did not care—had no choice, no purpose—is to blot out His benevolence, to nullify His wisdom, and convert His power into infinite indolence. To suppose that He did know, choose, and decree and that events do not accord with His purposes, is to suppose that God has made a world which He cannot govern, has undertaken a work too vast, has begun to build but is not able to finish. But to suppose that God did, from the beginning, behold all things open and naked before Him and that He did choose, with unerring wisdom and infinite goodness, how to govern His empire—and yet at the same time to employ heart and head and tongue in continual opposition to this great and blessed truth— is, most clearly, to cherish enmity to God and His government.

To object to the choice of God because it is immutable is to cavil against that which constitutes its consummating excellence. Caprice is a most alarming feature in a bad government; in a government absolutely perfect, none, surely, can object to its immutability but those who, if able, would alter it for the worse.

To say that there is no accountable agency in the conduct of His creatures because God always knew how to govern so as to display His glory, bless His kingdom, and always chooses thus to govern is to deny the possibility of a moral government, to contradict the express testimony of God and this too, at the expense of common sense and the actual experience of every subject of His moral government on earth.

Unconditional Submission Is Necessary

From the character of God and the nature of His government as explained in this discourse may be inferred the nature and necessity of unconditional submission to God.

Unconditional submission is an entire surrender of the

soul to God, to be disposed of according to His pleasure and occasioned by confidence in His character as God. There are many who would trust the Almighty to regulate the rolling of worlds and to rule in the armies of heaven just as He pleases; devils they would consign to His disposal without the least hesitation and their own nation, if they were sure that God would dispose of it according to their pleasure; even their own temporal concerns they would risk in the hands of God could they know that all things would work together for their good. Their souls, also, they would cheerfully trust to His disposal for the world to come if God would stipulate, at all events, to make them happy.

And to what does all this amount? Truly, that they care much about their own happiness and their own will but nothing at all about the will of God and the welfare of His kingdom. He may decree and execute His decrees in heaven and may turn its inhabitants into machines or uphold their freedom, as He pleases; apostate spirits are relinquished to their doom whether just or unjust. It is only when the government of God descends to particulars, draws near and enters their own selfish enclosures, claims a right to dispose of them, and extends its influence to the unseen world that selfishness and fear take the alarm. Has God determined how to dispose of my soul? Ah! that alters the case. If He can, consistently with freedom, govern angels, devils, and nations, how can He govern individuals? How can He dispose of me according to His eternal purpose and I be free? Here reason, all-penetrating and all-comprehensive, becomes weak; the clouds begin to collect, and the understanding, veiled by the darkness of the heart, can "find no end, in wandering mazes lost."

But if God has purposes of mercy in reserve for the sinner, he is convinced at length of his sin and finds himself in an evil case. He reforms, prays, weeps, resolves, and re-resolves, regardless of the righteousness of Christ and intent only to establish a righteousness of his own. But through all his windings sin cleaves to him, and the law with its fearful curse pursues him. Whither shall he flee? What shall he do? A rebel heart that will not bow fills him with despair. An angry God, who will not clear the guilty, fills him with terror. His strength is gone, his resources fail, his mouth is stopped. With restless anxiety or wild amazement, he surveys the gloomy prospect. At length, amidst the wanderings of despair, the character of God meets his eye. It is new, it is amiable and full of glory. Forgetful of danger, he turns aside to behold this great sight; while he gazes, new affections awake in his soul, inspiring new confidence in God and in His holy government. Now God appears qualified to govern, and now he is willing that He should govern and willing himself to be in the hands of God, to be disposed of according to His pleasure.

What is the occasion of this change? Has the divine character changed? There is no variableness with God. Did he, then, misapprehend the divine character? Was all this glory visible before? Or has a revelation of new truth been granted? There has been no new revelation. The character now admitted is the same which just before appeared so gloomy and terrible.

What, then, has produced this alteration? Has a vision of angels appeared to announce that God is reconciled? Has some sudden light burst upon him in token of forgiveness? Has Christ been seen upon the cross beckoning the sinner to come to Him? Has heaven been thrown open to his admiring eyes? Have enrapturing sounds of music stolen upon the ear to entrance the soul? Has some text of Scripture been sent to whisper that his sins are forgiven, though no repentance, faith, or love has dawned in his soul? And does he now submit because God has given him assurance of personal safety? None of these. Considerations of personal safety are, at the time, out of the question.

The change produced, then, is the effect of benevolence, raising the affections of the soul from the world and resting them upon God. Holiness is now most ardently loved. This is seen to dwell in God and His kingdom and to be upheld and perfected by His moral government. It is the treasure of the soul, and all the attributes of God stand pledged to protect it. The solicitude, therefore, is not merely, What will become of me? but, What, O Lord, will become of Your glory and the glory of Your kingdom? And in the character of God, these inquiries are satisfactorily answered. If God be glorified and His kingdom upheld and made happy, the soul is satisfied. There is nothing else to be anxious about; for individual happiness is included in the general good as the drop is included in the ocean.

The Unconquerable King

Charles Haddon Spurgeon (1834–1892) is undoubtedly the most famous minister of the last century. Converted in 1850, he united with the Baptists and soon began to preach in various places. He became pastor of the Baptist church in Waterbeach in 1851, and three years later he was called to the decaying Park Street Church, London. Within a short time, the work began to prosper, a new church was built and dedicated in 1861, and Spurgeon became London's most popular preacher. In 1855 he began to publish his sermons weekly, and today they make up the sixty-three volumes of *The Metropolitan Tabernacle Pulpit*. He founded a pastor's college and several orphanages.

This sermon is taken from *The Metropolitan Tabernacle Pulpit*, volume 16, and was preached on September 4, 1870, at the Metropolitan Tabernacle.

Charles Haddon Spurgeon

2

THE UNCONQUERABLE KING

At the end of the days I Nebuchadnezzar lifted up mine eyes unto heaven, and mine understanding returned unto me, and I blessed the most High, and I praised and honored him that liveth forever, whose dominion is an everlasting dominion, and his kingdom is from generation to generation: and all the inhabitants of the earth are reputed as nothing: and he doeth according to his will in the army of heaven, and among the inhabitants of the earth: and none can stay his hand, or say unto him, What doest thou? (Daniel 4:34–35).

No one has ever numbered Nebuchadnezzar with the prophets or believed his language to be inspired. We have before us simply a statement made by an uninspired man, after passing through the most extraordinary experience. He had been among the greatest and proudest of men. He suddenly fell into the condition of a grass-eating ox by losing his reason; upon being restored, he acknowledged publicly the hand of the Most High. I should not have taken his language as my text if it had not happened to be, as it is, a most correct and vigorous statement of sublime doctrines which are clearly stated by the Holy Spirit in different parts of Scripture. It is a singular instance of how, when God comes to deal with men in afflicting providences, He can make them clearly see many great truths concerning Himself and can constrain them to express their convictions in identically the same way as they would have done if His own Spirit had dictated the terms. There are certain parts of the divine character which even the unspiritual man cannot avoid seeing; after passing through certain processes of suffering and humiliation, the man is compelled to add his witness to the testimony of God's Spirit with regard to the divine character. Every single word that Nebuchadnezzar here utters can be backed up and supported by undoubtedly inspired words of men sent of God to proclaim infallible truth. We shall not therefore need to answer the objection that our text is simply the statement of Nebuchadnezzar—we grant that it is so—but we shall show as we proceed that Babylon's humbled monarch herein has spoken most correctly and accurately, and in full accordance with the testimony of other parts of Scripture.

Before I conduct your minds to a close consideration of the text, I must make one remark. Many of you will very naturally suppose that the chapter read during this service, the hymns, and the sermon were all intended to have reference to a certain great political event reported in the papers of last night.[1] But please to observe that your supposition will be unfounded, for my text was fixed upon yesterday morning before any sort of news had reached me, and the service would have been the same if that event had not occurred. So that anything strikingly suggestive in the choice of the passage may be looked upon, if you will, as denoting the guidance of God's Spirit but must not be imputed to any intentional reference on my part.

We will now come first to consider the doctrinal instruction of the text; secondly, we would learn the practical teaching of it; and thirdly, we would exhibit the spirit suitable after the contemplation of such a subject.

God's Self-existence

I. First, then, let us turn to the text, and consider THE DOCTRINAL INSTRUCTION here given to us.

We have here plainly stated the doctrine of *the eternal self-existence of God.* "I blessed the Most High, and I praised and honored him that liveth forever." If this word needed to be confirmed, we would refer you to the language of John in the Book of the Revelation, where we find him describing in the fourth chapter, at the ninth and tenth verses, the living creatures and the four and twenty elders

---

1. The overthrow of the government of Napoleon III of France during the Franco-Prussian War.

as giving glory and honor and thanks, "to him that sat on the throne, who liveth forever and forever." Better still, let us hear the witness of our own Redeemer in the fifth of John's gospel, at the twenty-sixth verse, where he declares that "the Father hath life in himself." My brethren, you need not that I marshal in array a host of confirmative passages for the eternal self-existence of God is taught throughout the Scriptures and is implied in that name which belongs only to the true God, Jehovah, "I AM that I AM." Where note that it is not "I was," which would imply that in some measure or respect He had ceased to be. Nor is it "I will be," which would intimate that He is not now what He will be; but I AM, the only being, the root of existence, the immutable and eternal One.

"We," as a venerable Puritan observes, "have more of nothing than of being," but it is God's prerogative to be. He alone can say, "I am God, and beside me there is none else." He declares, "I lift up my hand to heaven, and say I live forever." He is the one only underived, self-existent, self-sustained Being. Let us know of a surety that the Lord God whom we worship is the only Being who necessarily and from His own nature exists. No other being could have been but for His sovereign will, nor could it continue were that will suspended. He is the only light of life, all others are reflections that there should be any other intelligences. In all the future God must be. But the necessity for the continuance of other spirits lies in His will and not in the very nature of things. There was a time when the creatures were not. They came from Him as vessels from the potter's wheel. They all depend upon Him for continuance, as the streamlet on the fountain whence it flows; if it were His will they all would melt away as the foam upon the water. That immortality of spirits implied in such passages as Matthew 25:46, "These shall go away into everlasting punishment: but the righteous into life eternal," is the result of His own resolve to make spirits whose duration should be eternal. And though He will never withdraw the endowment of immortality which He has bestowed, yet the reason for eternal existence is not in the beings, but entirely in Himself, for essentially "he only hath immortality"—

He can create and He destroy.

All that is, whether material or intellectual, if so it had pleased God to ordain, might have been as transient as a sunbeam and have vanished as speedily as the rainbow from the cloud. If anything now exists of necessity, that necessity sprang from God and still depends upon the necessity of divine decree.

God is independent—the only being who is so. We must find food with which to repair the daily wastes of the body; we are dependent upon light and heat, innumerable external agencies, and above all and primarily dependent upon the outgoings of the divine power toward us. But the I AM is self-sufficient and all-sufficient.

> He sits on no precarious throne,
> Nor borrows leave to be.

He was as glorious before He made the world as He is now; He was as great, as blessed, divine in all His attributes before sun and moon and stars leaped into existence as He is now. If He should blot all out as a man erases the writing of his pen or as a potter breaks the vessel he has made, He would be nonetheless the supreme and ever-blessed God. Nothing of God's being is derived from another, but all that exists is derived from Him. You hills and mountains, you seas and stars, you men and angels, you heavens and you heaven of heavens—you minister nothing to Him who made you, but you all stand up together in existence flowing from your Creator.

God ever lives in this respect, that He undergoes no sort of change; all His creatures must from their constitution undergo more or less of mutation. Of them all it is decreed, "They shall perish, but thou shalt endure: yea, all of them shall wax old like a garment; as a vesture shalt thou change them, and they shall be changed: but thou art the same, and thy years shall have no end." Our life is made up of changes. From childhood we hasten to youth, from youth we leap to manhood, from manhood we fade into old age;

our changes are as many as our days. "The creature" is indeed in our case "made subject to vanity." Lighter than a feather, more frail than the flower of the field, brittle as glass, fleeting as a meteor, tossed to and fro like a ball, and quenched as a spark—"Lord, what is man?" There comes to us all in the time appointed the great and ultimate change in which the spirit is separated from the body, to be followed by another in which the divided manhood shall be reunited; with God there are no changes of this or any other kind. Has He not declared, "I am God, I change not"? God is essentially and evermore pure Spirit and consequently undergoes no variableness nor shadow of a turning. Of none of the creatures can this be said. Immutability is an attribute of God only. The things created were once new, they are waxing old, they will become older still; but the Lord has no time, He dwells in eternity. There is no moment of beginning with the Eternal, no starting point from which to calculate age. From of old He was the Ancient of Days, "from everlasting to everlasting thou art God." Let your mind retreat as far as its capacities will allow into the remote past of old eternity, and there it finds Jehovah alone in the fullness of His glory. Then let the same thought flash forward into the far-off future, as far as unreined imagination can bear it, and there it beholds the Eternal, unchanged, unchangeable. He works changes and effects changes, but He Himself abides the same. Brethren, let us worship Him with words like these—

Thy throne eternal ages stood,
Ere seas or stars were made;
Thou art the Ever-living God,
Were all the nations dead.

Eternity with all its years,
Stands present in thy view;
To thee there's nothing old appears;
Great God! there's nothing new.

Our lives through various scenes are drawn,
And vex'd with trifling cares,
While thine eternal thought moves on
Thine undisturb'd affairs.

That He lives forever is the result not only of His essential and necessary self-existence, of His independence, and of His unchangeableness, but of the fact that there is no conceivable force that can ever wound, injure, or destroy Him. If we were profane enough to imagine the Lord to be vulnerable, yet where is the bow and where is the arrow that could reach Him on His throne? What javelin shall pierce Jehovah's buckler? Let all the nations of the earth rise and rage against God, how shall they reach His throne? They cannot even shake His footstool. If all the angels of heaven should rebel against the Great King and their squadrons should advance in serried ranks to besiege the palace of the Most High, He has but to will it, and they would wither as autumn leaves or consume as the fat upon the altar. Reserved in chains of darkness, the opponents of His power would forever become mementos of His wrath. None can touch Him; He is the God that ever lives. Let us who delight in the living God bow down before Him and humbly worship Him, as the God in whom we live and move and have our being.

God's Everlasting Dominion

In our text we next find Nebuchadnezzar asserting *the everlasting dominion of God.* He says, "Whose dominion is an everlasting dominion, and His kingdom is from generation to generation." The God whom we serve not only exists but reigns. No other position would become Him but that of unlimited sovereignty over all His creatures. "The most high God, possessor of heaven and earth has prepared His throne in the heavens, and His kingdom rules over all." As David said, so also say we: "Thine, O Lord, is the greatness, and the power, and the glory, and the victory, and the majesty: for all that is in the heaven and in the earth is thine; thine is the kingdom, O Lord, and thou art exalted as head above all." "The Lord sitteth upon the flood; yea, the Lord sitteth King forever."

The Lord is naturally the ruler of all, but who shall pretend to rule over Him? He is not to be judged of man's finite reason, for He does great things which we cannot comprehend. Amazing is the impertinence of man when the creature dares to sit in judgment on the Creator. His character is not to be impugned or called in question; only the boundless arrogance of our pride would so dare to insult the thrice holy God. "Be still, and know that I am God," is a sufficient reply to such madness. The Lord's place is on the throne, and our place is to obey; it is His to govern, ours to serve; His to do as He wills, and ours, without questioning, to make that will our constant delight.

Remember, then, that in the universe God is actually reigning. Never let us conceive of God as being infinitely great, but not exerting His greatness, infinitely able to reign but as yet a mere spectator of events. It is not so. The Lord reigns even now. Though in one sense we pray, "Thy kingdom come," yet in another we say, "Thine is the kingdom, and the power, and the glory, forever and ever." The throne of the universe is not vacant nor its power in abeyance. God does not hold a bare title to kingship, but He is actually King. The government is upon His shoulders, the reins of management are in His hands.

Even at this hour He speaks to the sons of men, "See now that I, even I, am he, and there is no god with me: I kill, and I make alive; I wound, and I heal: neither is there any that can deliver out of my hand" (Luke 1:51–52). Before your very eyes He has fulfilled His word. Events appear to fly at random like the dust in the whirlwind, but it is not so. The rule of the Omnipotent extends over all things at all times. Nothing is left to its own chance hap, but in wisdom all things are governed. Glory be unto the omnipresent and invisible Lord of all.

This divine kingdom appeared very plainly to the once proud monarch of Babylon to be an everlasting one. The reign of the Everliving extends as other kingdoms cannot, "from generation to generation." The mightiest king inherits power and soon yields His scepter to His successor; the Lord has no beginning of days nor end of years; predecessor or successor are words inapplicable to Him. Other monarchies stand while their power is unsubdued, but in an evil hour a greater power may crush them down. There is no greater power than God; yea, there is no other power but that which proceeds from God, for "God hath spoken once. Twice have I heard this; that power belongs unto God"; hence His monarchy cannot be subdued, and must be everlasting. Dynasties have passed away, dying out for lack of heirs, but God the everliving asks none to succeed Him and to perpetuate aloft like forest trees, defiant of the storm. At the core the tree was rotten, and ere long, weakened by decay, it tottered to its fall; but the infinitely holy God has no injustice, error, partiality, or evil motive in the government of His affairs. Everything is arranged with spotless holiness, unimpeachable justice, unvarying fidelity, untarnished truth, amazing mercy, and overflowing love. All the elements of His kingdom are most conservative because they are radically right. There is no evil leaven in the council chamber of Omniscience, no corruption on the judgment-seat of heaven; hence "his throne is established in righteousness" (Ps. 47:8). Because His throne is holy we rejoice that it can never be moved.

Pause here, dear reader, and let your soul's eye behold again this view of things. God has reigned from the first day; God shall reign when days are gone. Everywhere He is the reigning God—reigning when Pharaoh said, "Who is Jehovah, that I should obey Him?" as much as when Miriam took her timbrel, and said, "Sing unto the Lord, for he hath triumphed gloriously"; reigning when Scribe and Pharisee, Jew and Roman nailed His only-begotten Son to the cross, as much as when the angelic cohorts shouted in triumph, "Lift up your heads, O ye gates, and be ye lift up, ye everlasting doors, that the King of Glory may come in"; reigning amid all the calamities which sweep the globe as much as He shall be in the halcyon days of peace. Never is the throne vacant, never is the scepter laid aside. Jehovah is always King and shall be King forever and forever. Oh, happy subjects, who have such a throne to look to! Oh, blessed children, who have such a King to be your Father! You, as a royal priesthood, may feel your royalties and your priesthoods both secure, for this unconquerable King sits securely on His throne. Your monarch has not yielded up His sword to a superior foe, you have not to search for another leader. In the person of His dear Son He walks among our golden candlesticks and holds our stars in His right hand. He keeps Israel and never slumbers nor sleeps.

Mankind's Nothingness

But we must hasten on. Nebuchadnezzar, humbled before God, uses in the third place extraordinary language with regard to *the nothingness of mankind.* "All the inhabitants of the earth are reputed as nothing." This is Nebuchadnezzar, but His words are confirmed by Isaiah, "Behold the nations are as a drop of a bucket," the unnoticed drop which remains in the bucket after it has been emptied into the trough or the drip which falls from it as it is uplifted from the well; a thing too inconsiderable to be worthy of notice. "And are counted as the small dust of the balance"; as the dust which falls upon scales, but is not sufficient to affect the balance in any degree whatever.

"Behold, he taketh up the isles as a very little thing." Whole archipelagos He uplifts as unconsidered trifles. This triple kingdom of ours He reckons not only to be little but "a very little thing." The vast island of Australia, the gems of the Pacific, the nations of the Southern Ocean, all these He handles as children lift their toys. "All nations before him are as nothing; and they are counted to him less than nothing and vanity." So if Nebuchadnezzar goes far, Isaiah, inspired of the Spirit, goes farther; the one calls the nations "nothing," and the other "less than nothing and vanity." You will find the passage in the fortieth of Isaiah at the fifteenth and seventeenth verses. Now mark the force of each word, "*all* the inhabitants of the earth," not some of them only, not the poor ones among them, but the rich, the kings, the wise, the philosophers, the priests, all put together, "are as nothing." What an assembly would there be if all the nations could be gathered together! An impressive spectacle rises before my vision! One has need possess an eagle's wing merely to pass over the mighty congregation. Where could a plain be found which could contain them all? Yet all of them, says the text, are "as nothing."

Now, observe they are so in themselves, for concerning all of us who are gathered here it is certain that there was a time when we were not—we were then in very deed "nothing." At this very moment, also, if God wills it, we may cease to be, and so in a step return to nothing. We are nothing in ourselves, we are only what He chooses to allow us to be, and when the time comes—and it will be a very short time, so far as this world is concerned—we shall be nothing. All that will remain of us among the sons of men will be some little hillock in a cemetery or a country churchyard for we shall have no part in anything which is done under the sun.

Of what account at this day, my brethren, are all the antediluvian millions? What are the hosts of Nimrod, of Shishak, of Sennacherib, or Cyrus? What wrecks the world of the myriads who followed the march of Nebuchadnezzar, who obeyed the beck of Cyrus, who passed away before the eye of Xerxes? Where are the generations which owned the sovereignty of Alexander or the legions which followed and almost adored the eagles of the Cæsars? Alas! even our grandsires, where are they? Our sons forewarn us that we must die. Have they not been born to bury us? So pass the generations like the successive series of forest leaves; what are they but as their best estate "altogether vanity"?

The nations are nothing in comparison with God. As you may place as many ciphers as you like together, and they all make nothing, so you may add up as many men, with all their supposed force and wisdom as you please, and they are all nothing in comparison with God. He is the unit. He stands for all in all and comprehends all; all the rest are but so many valueless ciphers till His unity makes them of account. Here let me remind you that every man who is spiritually taught of God is made to feel experimentally on his own account his own utter nothingness. When his inner eye, like that of Job, beholds the Lord, he abhors himself, he shrinks into the earth, he feels he cannot contrast or compare himself with the Most High even for a single second.

> Great God, how infinite art thou!
> What worthless worms are we!

This is the verse which naturally leaps to the lip of any man who knows himself and knows his God. Spiritually, our nothingness is very conspicuous. We were nothing in our election: "Ye have not chosen me, but I have chosen you"; "The children being not yet born, neither having done any good or evil, that the purpose of God according to election might stand, not of works, but of him that calleth"; "It is not of him that willeth, nor of him that runneth, but of God that showeth mercy." We were nothing in our redemption; we contributed nothing to that price which Jesus paid: "I have trodden the winepress alone; and of the people there was none with me." We are nothing in our regeneration. Can the spiritually dead help the blessed God to quicken them? "It is the Spirit that quickeneth, the flesh profiteth nothing." "We are his workmanship, created anew in Christ Jesus." We shall, when we get to heaven, make it part of our adoration to confess that we are less than nothing and vanity, but that God is all in all; therefore shall we cast our crowns at His feet and give Him all the praise forever and ever.

"The inhabitants of the earth are as nothing." It is a wonderful expression, and you see I do not attempt to expound it or any part of the text; I rather repeat words of the same meaning with the text by way of illustration. Before me is a great deep, and who shall fathom it? I would not darken counsel by words without knowledge.

If there were an ant's nest somewhere in a farmer's estate, suppose he had ten thousand acres of land, that ant's nest would bear some proportion, though a very small one, to the ten thousand acres of land. It could not be so strictly said to be as nothing as the whole world can when compared with God. This round earth bears a very insignificant proportion to the vast creation of God, even to that which is revealed to us by the telescope; we have reason to believe that all which can be seen with the telescope—if indeed it be a mass of worlds and all inhabited—is but as a pin's prick compared with the city of London to the far-reaching universe. If it be so and your mind were capable of compassing the entire creation of God, yet it would be only as a drop of a bucket compared with God Himself who made it all and could make ten thousand times ten thousand as much and then be but at the beginning of His power. This world then bears no such proportion to the Lord as an ant's nest to the estate of ten thousand acres.

Now if the farmer wishes to till the soil, it is not at all probable that he will take any cognizance whatever of that ant's nest in the arrangement of his affairs and in all probability will overturn and destroy it. This proves the insignificance of the emmet, and the greatness of man as compared with ants; but as it involves a degree of forgetfulness or overlooking on the farmer's part, the ants are great enough to be forgotten, but the nations are not great enough even for that. If it were possible by the farmer to arrange without difficulty all his plans so that without disturbing his proceedings every bird, emmet, and worm should be cared for in his scheme, how great then would he be compared with the ants! And this is just the case with the Lord. He so arranges all things, that apparently without effort the government of providence embraces all interests, wrongs none, but yields justice to all. Men are so little in the way of God that He never finds it needful to perpetrate an injustice even on a single man, and He has never caused one solitary creature to suffer one unnecessary pang.

Herein is His greatness, that it comprehends all littlenesses without a strain. The glory of His wisdom is as astonishing as the majesty of His power, and the splendors of His love and of His grace are as amazing as the terror of His sovereignty. He may do what He wills, for none can stay Him; but He never wills to do in any case aught that is unjust, unholy, unmerciful, or in any way inconsistent with the perfection of His matchless character. Here let us pause and worship. I at least must do so for my soul's eyes ache as though I had been gazing at the sun.

God's Sovereign Power

We turn now to the next sentence, which reveals *the divine power at work sovereignly.* "He doeth according to his will in the army of heaven, and among the inhabitants of the earth." This is easy to understand in reference to the celestial host, for we know that God's will is done in heaven. We devoutly pray that it may yet be done on earth after the same fashion. The angels find it their heaven to be obedient to the God of heaven. Under the term "army of heaven" is comprehended fallen angels who were once numbered with that band but were expelled from heaven for their rebellion. Devils unwillingly, but yet of necessity, fulfill the will of God. "Whatsoever the Lord pleased, that did in the heaven, and in earth, in the seas, and all deep places." When we read in the text that on earth God's will is done, we see that it is so in a measure among the righteous whose renewed hearts seek after God's glory. But the truth goes further, for that will is also accomplished in the unrighteous, and by those who know Him not. Yes, in those whose will is determined to oppose Him, still in some way unknown to us, the will of God is still achieved. (Prov. 19:21; Acts 4:27–28.)

I cannot understand a man taking so many pieces of wood and arranging them just as he pleases, nor can I see any very remarkable skill in so doing. But the miracle of divine glory lies in this—that He has made men free agents, has endowed them with a will, with which will He never interferes except according to the laws of mind; that He leaves them absolutely free to do what they will, and they will, universally of themselves, to do contrary to His will; yet, such is the magnificent strategy of heaven, such is the marvelous force of the divine mind, that despite everything, the will of God is done. Some have supposed that when we believe with David, in Psalm 115, that God has done whatsoever He has pleased, we deny free agency and, of necessity, moral responsibility also. Nay, but we declare that those who would do so are tinctured with the old captious spirit of him who said, "Why doth he yet find fault, for who hath resisted his will?" and our only answer is that of Paul, "Nay, but O man, who art thou that repliest against God?"

Can you understand it, for I cannot, how man is a free agent, a responsible agent, so that his sin is his own willful sin and lies with him and never with God; yet at the same time God's purposes are fulfilled, and His will is done even by demons and corrupt men? I cannot comprehend it. Without hesitation I believe it and rejoice so to do; I never hope to comprehend it. I worship a God I never expect to comprehend. If I could grasp Him in the hollow of mine hand, I could not call Him my God. If I could understand His dealings so that I could read them as a child reads his spelling book, I could not worship Him. But because He is so infinitely great, I find truth here, truth there, truth multiform; if I cannot compress it into one system, I know it is all clear to Him, and I am content that He should know what I know not. It is mine today to adore and obey. By-and-by when He sees fit, I shall know more and adore better. It is my firm belief that everything in heaven and earth and hell will be seen to be, in the long run, parts of the divine plan; yet never is God the author or the accomplice of sin, never is He otherwise than the hater of sin and the avenger of unrighteousness. Sin rests with man, wholly with man, and yet by some strange overruling force, Godlike and mysterious like the existence of God, His supreme will is accomplished.

Observe how the two truths combine in practice and are stated in the same verse in reference to our Lord's crucifixion in Acts 2:23: "Him, being delivered by the determinate council and foreknowledge of God, ye have taken, and by wicked hands have crucified and slain." Now, to deny this truth because we cannot understand it were to shut ourselves out of a great deal of important knowledge. Brethren, if God does not rule everywhere, then something rules where He does not, and so He is not omnipresently supreme. If God does not have His will, someone else does, and so far that someone is a rival to God. I never deny the free agency of man, or diminish his responsibility, but I dare never invest the free will of man with omnipotence, for this were to make man into a sort of god, an idolatry to be loathed.

Moreover, admit chance anywhere and you have admitted chance everywhere, for all events are related and act on one another. One cog of the wheel of providence disarranged or left to Satan or man's absolute freedom apart from God would spoil the whole machinery. I dare not believe even sin itself to be exempted from the control of providence or from the overruling dominion of the Judge of all the earth. Without providence we were unhappy beings; without the universality of the divine power, providence would be imperfect, and in some points we might be left unprotected and exposed to those evils which are by this theory supposed to be beyond divine control. Happy are we that it is true, "the Lord doeth as he wills in the army of heaven, and among the inhabitants of the earth."

God's Decrees Are Irresistible

Let us now consider the fifth part of the text—"None can stay his hand, or say unto him, What doest thou?" I gather from this *that God's fiat is irresistible and unimpeachable.* We are told by some annotators that the original has in it an allusion to a blow given to a child's hand to make him cease from some forbidden action. None can treat the Lord in that manner. None can hinder Him or cause Him to pause. He has might to do what He wills.

So also says Isaiah: "Woe unto him that strives with his Maker! Let the potsherd strive with the potsherds of the earth. Shall the clay say to him that fashioneth it, What makest thou? or thy work, He hath no hands?" (Isa. 45:9). Man is powerless, then, to resist the fiat of God. Usually he does not know God's design, although he blunderingly thinks he does. Often in opposing that apparent design, he fulfills the secret design of God against his will. If man did know God's design and should set himself with all his might against it, yet as the chaff cannot resist the wind, as it is not possible for the wax to resist the fire, so neither can man effectually resist the absolute will and sovereign good pleasure of the Most High.

Only here is our comfort; it is right that God should have this might, because He always uses His might with strictest rectitude. God cannot will to do anything unjust, ungenerous, unkind, ungodlike. No laws bind Him as they bind us, but He is a law to Himself. There is "Thou shalt," and "Thou shalt not," for me, for you, but who shall put "Thou shalt" to God, or who shall say, "Thou shalt not"?

Who shall attempt to be legislator for the King of kings? God is love. God is holiness. God is the law. God is love, and doing as He wills, He wills to love. God is holy, and doing as He wills, He wills holiness, He wills justice, He wills truth. Though there were raised a thousand questions—How is this just? How is that loving? How is that wise?—The one sufficient answer is—

> God is His own interpreter,
> And He will make it plain.

O sons of men, it is not for me to unriddle the enigmas of the Infinite—He shall explain Himself. I am not so impertinent as to be His apologist; He shall clear Himself. I am not called to vindicate His character. "Shall not the Judge of all the earth do right?" What folly to hold up a candle to show the brightness of the sun! How much more foolish to attempt to defend the thrice-holy Jehovah! Let Him speak for Himself if He will deign to contend with you. If you do but hear His thunders, how you tremble! When His lightnings set the heavens on fire, how amazed you are! Stand forth, then, and question Him if you dare. If you are at sea in a storm, when every timber of your vessel creaks, when the mast is broken, when the mariners stagger like drunken men, when overhead is the horrible tempest and the thundering voice of God in the tempest and all around you the howling winds, then you cease your cavilings and cry unto Him in your trouble. Act then this day as you would do in such a case, for you are equally in His hands (Ps. 99:1, 5; 100:3–4).

Thus have I tried to set forth the doctrine of the text.

A Practical Truth

II. Now, very briefly, consider its PRACTICAL INSTRUCTION.

I think the first lesson is, *how wise to be at one with Him!* As I bowed before the majesty of this text in my study, I felt within my soul, "Oh, how I long to be perfectly at one with this infinitely mighty, glorious, and holy God. How can I dare to be His enemy?" I felt then if I had not yielded before I must yield now, subdued before Him. I would that any of you who are not doing His will would

give up your hopeless rebellion. He invites you to come.
He might have commanded you to depart. In His infinite
sovereignty He has appointed Christ Jesus to be the Savior of men. Come and accept that Savior by faith.

*How encouraging this is to those who are at one with
God!* If He be on our side, who shall be against us? "The
Lord of Hosts is with us, the God of Jacob is our refuge."
We ought to be of the same mind as that believing woman
who, during an earthquake, was observed to be very happy. Everybody else was afraid—houses were falling, tow-
ers were rocking, but she smiled. When they asked her
why, she replied, "I am so glad to find that my God can
shake the world; I believed He could, and now I see that
He can." Be glad that you have One to trust in to whom
nothing is impossible, who can and will achieve His purposes. My heart feels that she would give Him the power
if He had it not, and if it were all mine, I would leave all
power in His hands even if I could remove it. "Great God,
reign thou supremely, for there is none like unto thee."
"The Lord reigneth; let the earth rejoice; let the multitude
of isles be glad thereof."

How joyful this thought ought to be *to all holy workers!*
You and I have enlisted on the side of God and of His
Christ, and though the powers against us seem very strong,
yet the invincible King will surely put them to the rout
ere long. Romanism, idolatry, infidelity, these all appear
mighty things—so seem those pots fresh from the potter—a child thinks them to be stone. But when the Lord
Jesus smites them with the rod of iron, see how the potsherds fly! This shall He do ere long. He will lift the
might of His terrible arm and bring down His iron rod;
then shall it be seen that the truth as it is in Jesus must
and shall prevail.

How this should *help you that suffer!* If God does it all,
and nothing happens apart from God, even the wickedness
and cruelty of man being still overruled by Him, you readily may submit. How graciously and with what good face
can you kiss the hand which smites you! The husband is
gone to heaven, God took him; the property has melted,
God has permitted it. You were robbed, you say; well, think

not so much of the second cause, look to the great first cause. You strike a dog, he bites the stick; if he were wise, he would look at you who use it. Do not look at the second cause of the afflictions, look to the great first cause; it is your God who is in it all, your Father God, the infinitely good. Which would you desire to have done on earth, your will or God's will? If you are wise, you say, "Not my will, but thine be done." Then accept the ways of providence. Since God appoints them, accept them with grateful praise. Herein is true sacrifice to God when we can say, "Though he slay me, yet will I trust in him." We have received good at His hands, and we have blessed Him—heathen men and publicans might have done that; if we receive evil and still bless Him, this is grace, this is the work of His Holy Spirit. If we can bow before His crushing strokes and feel that if the crushing of us by the weight of His hand will bring Him honor, we are content; this is true faith. Give us grace enough, O Lord, never to fail in our loyalty but to be Your faithful servants even to suffering's bitterest end. Oh, to have the mind thus subjected to God! Some kick at the doctrine of divine sovereignty, but I fear it is because they have a rebellious, unhumbled spirit. Those who feel obedient to God cannot have God cried up too much, cannot yield Him too absolute an authority. Only a rebellious child in a house wishes the father to be tied by rules and regulations. No, my Father must do right; let Him do what He wills.

A Proper Response

III. What is THE RIGHT SPIRIT in which to contemplate all this?

The first is *humble adoration*. We do not worship enough, my brethren. Even in our public gatherings we do not have enough worship. O worship the King! Bow your heads now—bow your spirits rather and adore Him that lives forever and ever. Your thoughts, your emotions—these are better than bullocks and he-goats to be offered on the altar. God will accept them. Worship Him with lowliest reverence, for you are nothing, and He is all in all.

Next let the spirit of your hearts be that of *unquestion-*

ing acquiescence. He wills it! I will do it or I will bear it. God help you to live in perfect resignation.

Next to that, exercise the spirit of *reverent love.* Do I tremble before this God? Then I must seek more grace that I may love Him as He is; not love Him when my thoughts have diminished Him of His splendor and robbed Him of His glory, but love Him even as an absolute sovereign for I see that sovereignty exercised through Jesus Christ, my shield and His Anointed. Let me love my God and King, and be a courtier, happy to be admitted near His throne, to behold the light of the Infinite Majesty.

Lastly, let our spirit be that of *profound delight.* I believe there is no doctrine to the advanced Christian which contains such a deep sea of delight as this. The Lord reigns! The Lord is King forever and ever! Why, then all is well. When you get away from God, you get away from peace. When the soul dives into Him and feels that all is in Him, then she feels calm delight, a peace like a river, a joy unspeakable. Strive after that delight this morning, my beloved, and then go and express it in your songs of praise. If you are alone this afternoon, any of you, and not engaged in service, be sure to bless and magnify your God. Lift up your hearts in His praise, for "whoso offereth praise glorifieth God."

May the Lord bring us all, through faith in Jesus Christ, into harmony with this ever-blessed and ever-living God, and unto Him be praise and glory forever and forever. Amen.

Are You Criticizing God?

Reuben Archer Torrey (1856–1928) was one of America's best-known evangelists and Bible teachers. Educated at Yale and various German universities, he went through a time of skepticism from which he emerged a staunch preacher of the faith. In 1889 D. L. Moody called Torrey from the pastorate to become superintendent of his new school in Chicago, now the Moody Bible Institute. He also served as pastor of the Chicago Avenue Church, now the Moody Church. He and Charles Alexander conducted evangelistic meetings together in many parts of the world. From 1912 to 1919, Torrey served as dean of the Bible Institute of Los Angeles. He served from 1914 as pastor of the Church of the Open Door. From 1924 to his death, he ministered in conferences and taught at the Moody Bible Institute.

This sermon is from *R. A. Torrey* in the "Great Pulpit Masters" series, originally published in 1950 by Fleming H. Revell.

Reuben Archer Torrey

3

ARE YOU CRITICIZING GOD?

O man, who art thou that repliest against God? (Romans 9:20).

THESE WORDS ought to awaken anyone who is not utterly beyond hope. Notice the first two words and the last word. "O man" and "God." "O man, who art thou that repliest against God?" Here God and man are put in sharpest contrast, God in His infinite greatness and wisdom and man in his infinitesimal smallness and ignorance. And in the Greek there is also a strong emphasis on the "thou." "O MAN, who art thou that repliest against GOD?" It will be a happy day for some of us if God will brand that text upon our memories so that we shall never be able to forget it nor get away from it. "O man, who art thou that repliest against God?"

The most insanely daring thing that any man can do, the most exceedingly foolish thing any man can do, the most desperately wicked thing that any man can do, is to reply against God, to enter into controversy with God, to criticize God, to condemn God. Yet that is what many people are doing.

When you hear a little child replying against his father or mother, getting into controversy, criticizing, condemning, you are filled with disgust and indignation. It is something not to be tolerated for one moment. But what is it for any mere human being, any mere creature of the dust such as all of us are, to reply against, to criticize, to enter into controversy with, to try to prove wrong the Infinite and Eternal God? It is the most exceedingly foolish and desperately wicked thing a human being can do.

I. The Folly and Wickedness of Entering into Controversy with God

There are four facts which show the exceeding folly and desperate wickedness of replying against God, of

45

entering into controversy with God, of criticizing or condemning God.

The first is the fact of the infinite majesty of God. Our text itself contrasts the infinite majesty of God with the infinitesimal smallness of man. It reads, "O man, who art thou that repliest against God?" Yes, who art thou, anyway? And who is God?

You are one out of 2,000,000,000 like yourself now inhabiting this globe. And what is this globe on which you and I live? The earth is so small a part of the already known universe that if the sun were hollow, you could pour into it 1,200,000 earths like ours and still there would be room enough left for them to rattle around in it.

Yes, the sun itself is very, very small in comparison with Arcturus and some of the other stars whose diameters have been recently measured, and there are now known to be more than 225,000,000 of these great worlds we call stars in this universe of ours. God, with whom you are seeking to enter into controversy, seeking to criticize and condemn, made them all. "He made the stars also" (Gen. 1:16). "O man, who art thou that repliest against God?"

We men in this day of increasingly successful investigation of the incredible, and, as it seems to us, practically infinite, magnitude of the stellar heavens are sometimes tempted to be puffed up because a few great leaders and investigators among us are beginning to know a little about these vast stellar worlds and interstellar spaces. But what about the God who planned them all and made them all? Our increasing discoveries of the vastness of the physical universe ought to fill us with an increasing sense of our own nothingness in comparison with the infinite greatness and majesty of Him who planned and made them all. But, alas, oftentimes it seems only to puff us up with pride that we are so wise as to understand a small part of the ways and power of yon infinite God.

The second fact that shows us the exceeding folly and desperate wickedness of replying against God, of entering into controversy with God, of criticizing God, of condemning God, is the fact of the infinite and absolute holiness of God. "God is light, and in him is no darkness at all" (1 John 1:5). God is the One, as I read in the Scripture lesson tonight, in whose presence the seraphim themselves, the "burning ones" (for that is what the Hebrew word "seraphim" means), burning in their own intense holiness, must veil their faces and feet in that infinitely holy Presence and keep continually crying, "Holy, holy, holy, is the Lord God Almighty" (Isaiah 6:3). God is the One in whose presence Isaiah, that holy man of old, covered his face and cried, "Woe is me! for I am undone; for I am a man of unclean lips, and I dwell in the midst of a people of unclean lips, . . . for mine eyes have seen the King, Jehovah of hosts." God is the One in whose presence Job, the "perfect man," Job, who had stoutly maintained his integrity before all the persistent and united accusations of his friends, when he got one glimpse of God face to face, overwhelmed with the sense of his own nothingness and vileness in comparison with the infinitely holy One, cried, "I have heard of thee with the hearing of the ear: but now mine eye seeth thee. Wherefore I abhor myself, and repent in dust and ashes" (Job 42:5–6). Such is God. And "who art thou that repliest against God?" And what art thou?

What are we all, the very best of us? Vile—the best of us is but a loathsome sinner. We may not yet realize the fact, but it is true. Our lives have been shot through and through by sin. Yet you undertake to stand in the presence of this Holy God, in whose presence the seraphim veil their faces and their feet, and reply against Him, to suggest what God ought to do, to enter into controversy with God, to criticize God for things which He has seen fit to do, to murmur against God.

There is a third fact that shows us the exceeding folly and desperate wickedness of replying against God, of entering into controversy with God, of criticizing God, of condemning God, and that is the fact of God's infinite wisdom. God is not only a Being of infinite majesty and holiness. He is also a Being of infinite wisdom. We look up at the starry heavens above our heads, we look at these wonderful worlds of light that stud the heavens by night. We think of the overwhelming things about their immensity and the incredible speed and momentum of their movements as they rush through space, and as we look up at them, if we are wise, we say, "Oh, God, what a Being of infinite wisdom as well as majesty Thou art that Thou canst guide these inconceivably enormous worlds as they go whirling through space with such incredible velocity and momentum."

And yet many of you here tonight do not hesitate to look up at that infinitely wise God who made these wonderful spheres of light, who guides the whole universe in its wonderful, stupendous and bewildering course, and attempt to tell Him what you think He ought to do! Thou fool, art thou mad? No inmate of Patten ever did an insaner thing. "Who art thou?" The wisest man on earth is but a child; the wisest philosopher does not know much; the greatest man of science knows but very little. What he knows is almost nothing in comparison with what he does not know. What he does know, even about the material universe, is as nothing compared with what he does not know.

How much does the wisest scientist know even about this small planet? What does he really know, for example, about earthquakes? Have you ever stopped to think of the fact that the most confidently believed science of one hundred years ago is regarded by all modern scientists as foolishness? If we are to judge the future by the past, the most confidently believed science of today will be regarded as foolishness by the scientists of one hundred years hence.

When I was giving special attention to scientific study not so very many years ago, the nebular hypothesis was almost universally accepted. But some of the most advanced and reliable scientists of today are not only questioning it, but declare, at least in private, that it is exploded. What the scientists of a hundred years ago taught as being settled forever is known by our little children in the primary schools today as completely disproven. What the best scientist of today thinks he knows to be true a little child in primary school one hundred years hence will know to be false. The best scientific knowledge of today will be regarded as foolishness a hundred years from now, and the best scientific knowledge of one hundred years from now will be foolishness to the Infinitely wise God.

Suppose some child of thirteen or fourteen should take a book on philosophy setting forth the ripest product of the best philosophic thought of today and begin to criticize it, page by page. What would you think? Would you stand and look at the boy and say with unbounded admiration, "What a bright lad he is?" No, you would say, "What a conceited idiot he is to undertake, at his age and with his limited knowledge, to criticize the best philosophic thought of the day!" But he would not be so conceited an idiot as you or I would be were we to attempt to criticize an infinitely wise God for we are far less than children compared with the infinite God.

The most profound philosopher of today is but a little child compared with the Infinite God. And yet you, who do not make any pretensions of being a philosopher at all, take God's Book, you a little child, an infant, take this Book which represents the best wisdom of God, and you sit down and turn it, page by page, and try to criticize it, and people stand and look at you and admire and say, "What a scholar!" But the angels look down and say, "What a fool!" And what does God say? "O man, who art thou that repliest against God?" "He that sitteth in the heavens shall laugh; the Lord [the Almighty and the Eternal] shall have [you] in derision" (Ps. 2:4).

There is a fourth fact that emphasizes the extreme folly and desperate wickedness of replying against God, of entering into controversy with God, of criticizing God, or condemning God, and that fact is that He is not only a Being of Infinite majesty, holiness, and wisdom, but also a Being of infinite goodness and love. Why, man, you owe everything you have in the world to God. You owe your very existence to Him. You owe to Him your power to see, your power to hear, your power to taste. You owe to Him your power to breathe, to live, to walk, to work, your power to enjoy this wonderful world which He has made, in which He permits and enables us to live. "Every good gift and every perfect gift is from above, and cometh down from the Father of lights, with whom is no variableness, neither shadow of turning" (James 1:17). The poorest of us, the most unfortunate of us, has an immense deal for which to be thankful. You who seem to have very little have exceedingly much in comparison with nothing. Are you blind? Well, you can hear and taste, can you not? Are you deaf, dumb, and blind? Well, you can eat and enjoy your food, can you not? The man who has all five senses would be just as reasonable if he were to complain because he has not six as the man who has four senses would be to complain because he has not five. Thank God for what you have, rather than complain against God for what you have not.

Suppose I should have found on Thanksgiving Day a poor, half-starved tramp and had taken him to my home, given him a good, well-cooked dinner of roast lamb, white potatoes, other vegetables, and pumpkin pie, and then he had gone and complained against me to some other tramp because I did not give him turkey and sweet potatoes, cranberry sauce, mince pie, and plum pudding. Would he not have been an ungrateful cur? Yet not so ungrateful as you are when you complain at the God who has given you taste, hearing, touch, feeling, and many other blessings, because He has not given you sight also. The poorest of us, the most suffering of us, have an enormous deal for which to be thankful and all of it came from God. Not only that, but you and I not only have these things that we possess to be thankful for but, furthermore, every man of us has trampled God's law under foot; every one of us has been a sinner justly condemned before God. But God, instead of dealing with us in stern wrath and judgment, as we all deserve, has not only given us all these blessings, but, in addition, has given His own Son to die on the Cross of Calvary in our place. He has given His best beloved, His dearest, His only begotten Son. But in spite of all that wondrous love that did not stop even at the sacrifice of His own Son, some of you presume to criticize God, who gave His Son to die for you. "O man, who art thou that repliest against God?"

One of the greatest Italian statesmen of the last century, the greatest of his day but one, was devoutly loved in his youth by a young woman. When he entered the army of Garibaldi, this woman who loved him enlisted too, and fought in the war by the side of her lover, just to be near him. And one day he was shot and fell on the field of battle, and that woman who loved him rushed out beneath a rain of bullets, lifted her fallen lover from the ground; and, amidst a terrific storm of bullets, carried her lover to safety. Then she watched over him for days and weeks until she had nursed him back to health. Suppose he had deserted her then, what would the whole world have called him? In point of fact he married her, but afterward he divorced her; though he was one of the ablest statesmen of the century, Italy and all Europe, for all his brilliant gifts, never forgave him his treatment of the devoted woman who had risked her life to save his.

But what has God done for you? The eternal God has consented that His heart should be torn and crushed to save you and me. Yet some of us dare to enter into controversy with this God of infinite love, to criticize that eternal God who consented that His heart be torn and bruised and crushed to save us. Oh, the desperate wickedness, the amazing folly of replying against a God of infinite majesty, infinite holiness, infinite wisdom, and, above all, of infinite love. "O man, who art thou that repliest against God?"

II. Who Repliest Against God?

But who is replying against God? Who is entering into controversy with God? Who is criticizing or condemning God? Five classes are replying against God.

First of all, the men and women who complain of God's providential dealings with them are replying against God, are entering into controversy with God, are criticizing

God and condemning God. Many a man or woman has said to me, "I think God is cruel." "Why do you think He is cruel?" One replies, "He has taken away my husband." Another, "He has taken away my wife." Another, "He has taken away my child. He has taken away the light of our home." Another, "He has brought me down from financial prosperity to financial failure. I once stood high in the business world. I now have to almost beg my bread, and I say God is cruel." Another says, "If God is good, why did He permit this awful disaster or that which laid waste a beautiful city or nation? I think God is cruel."

You do? You do? You think God is cruel! Who is God? A Being of infinite majesty, a Being of infinite holiness, a Being of infinite wisdom, a Being of infinite love, a Being who gave His own Son to die that you might be saved! "O man, who art thou that repliest against God?"

But you say, "I do not understand it." Why should you understand it? Who are you? If you were really wise, you would not ask to understand it. If you had really good sense, you would not feel any need of having it explained. You would say, "I know God is infinitely good and infinitely wise. I know He is infinitely loving, too. I know He gave His Son to die for me, and though I cannot understand it, nevertheless it comes from God's hand and I know it is all right. "Naked came I [into this world]: . . . the Lord gave, and the Lord hath taken away; blessed be the name of the Lord" (Job 1:21). I do not ask to understand; I am perfectly content to trust in the dark that God who is so infinitely worthy of my trust.

I had two friends in England, very dear friends, who were beautiful Christians. They had a lovely daughter. She grew to maidenhood and was said to have been an unusually beautiful girl in both face and character. Some said she was the most beautiful character they had ever met. When this lovely daughter was seventeen or eighteen, she was taken with rheumatic fever, and, after awful suffering, died. The father and mother never complained. They kissed the hand that smote.

Some time after this sorrow had befallen them, I was talking with them about it. They told me how God had sustained them in that trying hour. Only a little while after this conversation, their second daughter, now grown to womanhood, was also taken down with precisely the same malady, rheumatic fever. Her fever ran up to 107 and stayed there day after day, and she seemed beyond all hope. Then the mother's faith gave way, and she said, "God is cruel to take my second daughter when I never complained about the first, and not only to take my second daughter, but to take her in just the same way He took the first." But God spared the child. She is well now, a devoted Christian woman in very active Christian work. And that mother has repented of her wickedness.

Oh, friends, it was wicked, very wicked. Our hearts were almost broken in sympathy during the days that child hung between life and death. Telegrams kept coming to me telling of her condition, and my heart bled for my friends. But, nonetheless, I say that was wicked on the mother's part to say "God is cruel." That was exceedingly wicked, that was desperately wicked, to call God cruel. That same mother lost all three of her sons and her husband in the late war, but she has never again whispered that God is cruel. I had a letter from her only the other day that was full of trust and hope.

Some of you are passing through trials which, if the rest of us knew, would fill our hearts with sympathy and pain. But you are murmuring against God, and that is wicked, that is exceedingly foolish, that is desperately wicked; for "O man, who art thou that repliest against God," against a God of infinite majesty, against a God of infinite wisdom, against a God of infinite holiness, against a God of infinite love, against a God who gave His only begotten Son to die for you? But you say, "I do not understand it." Why should you understand it? Why should you ask to understand it? Who are you that God should explain it to you? Oh, that we might always bear in mind who God is, and who we are; what God is, and what we are.

Then there is a second class who are replying against God, who are entering into controversy with God, who are criticizing and condemning God, namely, those who are criticizing this Book and trying to pull this Book to pieces. This Book is God's Word. That is thoroughly established. When you criticize this Book, you criticize its Author, who is God. When you criticize this Book, you criticize God. But you say, "I do not believe it is God's Word." That does not alter the fact, not in the least. It is His Word—there is abundant proof that it is His Word. I have proved over and over again in this place that this Book is the Word of God. This Book is God's Word, and whoever ventures to criticize it ventures to criticize God. Never forget that. I repeat it, whoever ventures to criticize this Book ventures to criticize God, and the one who criticizes God is guilty of exceeding folly and desperate wickedness. You say, "I do not like that." I am sorry that you do not, for it is true, and I always feel profoundly sorry for the man or woman who does not like the truth. They are in a bad way.

One night one of my workers in Minneapolis called me down to speak to a man who said that he was an infidel. "Why are you an infidel?" I asked. "Because I do not believe the Bible," he replied. "Yes, but why do you not believe the Bible?" "It is full of contradictions," he answered. "Show me one," I quietly said, and handed him my Bible to find it. He said, "It is full of them." "Well," I said, "if it is full of them, you ought to be able to show me at least one." "I don't pretend to know as much about the Bible as you do," he blurted out. I said, "Then what are you talking about it for?" I turned him to our Bible text of tonight, "O man, who art thou that repliest against God?" Then I turned him to Matthew 12:36, "Every idle word that men shall speak, they shall give account thereof in the day of judgment." Then I said, "The Bible is God's Word, and you have said it is full of contradictions, and in saying that you have condemned the Author, you have condemned God, and Jesus said, 'Every idle word that men shall speak, they shall give account thereof in the day of judgment.' You have criticized God, and you will have to give account of it in the day of judgment, of all these words, these idle words that you have just used." He turned pale, and said, "I did not mean to do that." "But that is what you have done." And it is what some of you have done in the last twenty-four hours. You have ventured to laugh at something in the Bible. When you did that, you laughed at God. You ventured to set up some opinion of yours against what God says in His Book. You ventured to enter into controversy with God, you ventured to criticize something in the Bible, and when you did that, you criticized the Author of the Bible, you criticized God. "O man, who art thou that repliest against God?"

There is a third class who are replying against God, who are entering into controversy with God, who are criticizing God, who are condemning God, and that is those who make light of the Bible doctrine of salvation by atoning blood, the Bible doctrine that we are saved through the shedding of the blood of Jesus on the Cross of Calvary. That doctrine so frequently and so unmistakably taught in God's Word is ridiculed today in many a so-called Christian pulpit. Any pulpit that ridicules the doctrine of salvation by atoning blood is not a Christian pulpit.

A very noted preacher in New York City, whose books have a wide sale, was reported to me by one who took down his words in his classroom to have said, "The doctrine of blood atonement is nauseating to me." Any preacher who ridicules the doctrine of salvation by atoning blood is not a minister of Jesus Christ, he is a minister of Satan, no matter how genial and amiable a man he may be.

The Bible doctrine of salvation by atoning blood is ridiculed in this day on every hand. Some preachers have said it is foolish for me to preach this "old doctrine." Well, it is an old doctrine, but it is a true doctrine. And I would rather believe and teach the old that is true than the new that is false. I did not invent this doctrine. I do not know enough to invent it. I found it in that Book, and, thank God, I found it to be true in my own life; it saved me and I preach it, and it has saved thousands through my preaching of it. I preach it, but I did not invent it. God is the Author of this doctrine, and when you criticize the preaching of it, you do not criticize me, you criticize God. It would be a matter of no great consequence for you to criticize me or my preaching. Why should you not criticize me? I am not infallible. I cannot see why I am not just as

properly an object of criticism as anybody else. It does not
harm me, and it gives some people lots of fun. Sometimes
it greatly helps me. But, ah, when you criticize this doctrine you are not criticizing me, you are criticizing God,
and that is serious, tremendously serious. "O man, who
art thou that repliest against God?"

Then there is a fourth class who are replying against
God, namely, those who complain of the Bible doctrine of
retribution for sin, the Bible doctrine of endless punishment. This is not my doctrine. I did not get it up. Some
say that it is a medieval doctrine. No, it is not a medieval
doctrine. They did not originate it in the Middle Ages. It
is the doctrine of Jesus Christ, taught by Him, not in the
Middle Ages but in the first century. Why will people who
try to pose as scholars display such ignorance of the meaning of commonly used words?

Jesus Christ says distinctly in Matthew 25:41 that at
the judgment of the nations living on the earth when He
comes again He will say to those on His left hand, "Depart from me, ye cursed, into the everlasting fire, prepared for the devil and his angels." And, five verses farther
down, He says, "And these shall go away into eternal
punishment: but the righteous into life eternal." Now, I
did not invent that. That was in the Bible before I was
born. Jesus said it eighteen centuries before I was born. I
simply found it in the Bible and preach it because it is
there. I received a letter once from a Universalist preacher in New Hampshire, saying, "The doctrine you preach
makes God a monster." Whoever says that this doctrine
makes God a monster is himself a blasphemer, for it is
God's doctrine. When you say that "Whosoever preaches
this doctrine makes God a monster," you say that God is a
monster. A lady in Liverpool wrote me, "I cannot conceive
how a God of love should leave anybody to everlasting
punishment." Why should she conceive how a God of love
should leave anybody to everlasting punishment? It seemed
to have never entered her head that anything she could
not conceive could be easily conceivable by someone who
knew more than she did. If she had had even a modicum

of commonsense, she would have seen at once that although she, with her very limited intelligence, could not conceive it, an infinitely wise God might have a thousand reasons for doing it, even though she could not see one. It has never dawned on some people that even God could by any possibility know more than they know. It never dawned on me for years, and in those days I was a Universalist. I thought that all men would ultimately be saved. I was a Universalist because I had an argument for the ultimate salvation of everybody for which I could see no possible answer. I thought if I could not see an answer, why, no one could. So I challenged anybody to meet me on that argument and answer it. I went around with my head pretty high and said, "I have found an unanswerable reason for Universalism." I thought that I was a Universalist for all time and that anyone who was not a Universalist was not well posted.

One day it occurred to me that an infinitely wise God might possibly know more than I did. That had never dawned on me before. It dawned upon me also that it was quite possible that a God of infinite wisdom might have a thousand good reasons for doing a thing, when I, in my finite foolishness, could not see even one. So my fondly cherished Universalism went up in smoke.

If you get that thought, that an infinitely wise God may possibly know more than even you do, and that God in His infinite wisdom might have a thousand good reasons for doing a thing when you cannot see even one, you will have learned one of the greatest theological truths of the day—one that will solve many of your perplexing problems in the Bible.

Men try to lay hold of infinite wisdom and fancy that they can squeeze it down into the capacity of their pint-cup minds. But because they cannot squeeze infinite wisdom into their pint-cup minds, they say, "I don't believe that Book is the Word of God, because it has something in it that I cannot understand the philosophy of." Why should you understand the philosophy of it? Who are you, anyhow? How much of a mind have you, anyhow? How long have you had it? How long are you going to keep it? Who gave it to you?

It is not our business to find out the philosophy of things; it is not our business to see the reason of things. It is our business to hear what God has to say, and when He says it, believe it, whether you can understand the philosophy of it or not.

When my children were small and ignorant, I told them a lot of things that I could not explain to them because of the limitations of their minds. There are a great many things that even God cannot explain to you or to me because we do not know enough yet to have it explained to us. God is too wise, I say it reverently, to try to explain some things to a person who does not know more than you do.

There is one more class that is replying against God, that is the men who instead of accepting Jesus Christ as their Savior and surrendering to Him as their Lord and Master and openly confessing Him as such before the world, are making excuses for not doing it. Jesus says in John 6:37, "Him that cometh to me I will in no wise cast out." God says in Revelation 22:17, "Whosoever will, let him take the water of life freely." Anybody can come to Christ, and anybody who does come will be received and saved. Yet many of you, instead of coming, are making excuses for not coming. By every excuse you make you are replying against God, you are entering into controversy with God, you are condemning God, who invites you to come. You cannot frame an excuse for not coming and accepting Christ that does not condemn God. Every excuse that any mortal makes for not accepting Christ, in its ultimate analysis, condemns God.

For example, some of you say, "I am too great a sinner to come." But God says in 1 Timothy 1:15, "This is a faithful saying, and worthy of all acceptation, that Christ Jesus came into the world to save sinners." And when you say, "I cannot come because I am too great a sinner," you give the lie to God. He says you can.

Another says, "I cannot come because I am too weak to hold out in the Christian life." But God says in Jude 24, "He is able to keep you from falling and to present you faultless before the presence of his glory with exceeding joy." You say, "God cannot keep me." God says He can. And when you say He cannot, you make God a liar and condemn God. Another says, "I cannot come because I have not the right kind of feeling." But God says, "Whosoever will, let him come and take the water of life freely." God says, "You can come," and you say, "I cannot," and that excuse condemns God. Every conceivable excuse the sinner makes for not coming to Christ at once, in its ultimate analysis, condemns God, and every man and woman who, instead of coming right to the Lord Jesus and accepting Him, surrendering to Him, confessing Him as Master and going forth to serve Him—everyone who is making an excuse of any kind instead of accepting Christ is replying against God. "O man, who art thou that repliest against God?"

God and History

William Graham Scroggie (1877–1958) was born in England of Scottish parents who were active as evangelists. After a few years in the business world, he felt a call to ministry and spent three years in Spurgeon's College, London, and devoted himself to the mastery of the English Bible. He served in five pastorates, the most notable being Charlotte Chapel, Edinburgh (1916–1933) and Spurgeon's Tabernacle, London (1938–1944). He was the author of many books, including the *Know Your Bible* series, *The Unfolding Drama of Redemption* (three volumes), and *A Guide to the Gospels*. He ministered the Word throughout the United Kingdom as well as in the United States, Canada, Australia, and New Zealand.

This address was originally published in the *Charlotte Chapel Record* of 1927.

William Graham Scroggie

4

GOD AND HISTORY

Now faith is the substance of things hoped for, the evidence of things not seen. . . . Through faith we understand that the worlds were framed by the word of God, so that things which are seen were not made of things which do appear (Hebrews 11:1, 3).

WE ARE TO understand that the worlds were framed by the Word of God through faith. Living as we are in one of the most momentous periods of human history, it becomes all thoughtful people to endeavor, at least, to relate the past to the present and the present to the future, and all things to God. Our subject, therefore, is God and history.

I wish to consider, first of all, the action of God in history and then His method. In considering the action of God in history, we must think first of the historic building and then of the Divine Builder. In considering the historic building, I ask your attention to three things: first, the meaning of these words, "The worlds were framed by God"; in the second place, to the fact of dispensations; and in the third place, to the unit of history. All that in considering the historic building.

It might be supposed by a reading of this verse that it is material worlds that we are referring to. Perhaps the primary reference is to creation and to the first chapter of Genesis; the word here used, *worlds* or *ages,* is extended into faith in the growing process of God's perfect world. A moral purpose enters into creation. No doubt the troubled days of the people to whom this letter was written led them to think of history as disorderly, and the ways of God put them to intellectual perplexity. The writer, therefore, would reassure them and steady their faltering faith. Time-worlds, therefore, are here in view, not matter-worlds. What is referred to is some of the periods of time, including all that is manifested in them and through them.

The order which exists through time is developed in successive stages or cycles of universal life; for the significant element in creation is not the mass or magnificence of the material spheres but the evolution of God's purpose through the ages. The mind staggers in its endeavor to grasp the vastness of the physical universe. And much more overwhelming is the thought that these time periods and periods and ages in which the purpose of God is evolving is in the process of being fulfilled, unhasting and unresting in the boundless life which He has called into being. Let us read the passage, therefore, in this light. "By faith we understand the ages to have been formed by the word of God."

The House of History

Thus we see that God is the builder of human history. In some quarters the word "ages" is more acceptable than the word "dispensations." There are some people who think that the whole conception of *dispensation* originated with the Plymouth Brethren. But no! It is as old as divine revelation; it is as old as human history; and there is a deep and profound necessity for such dispensations. That time-worlds are meant by the writer seems clear from the fact that he immediately proceeds to speak not of the material universe, not of the wonders of this great cosmos upon which we live, but of human history and that in its successive stages—more especially, the history of his own people, for observe that the chapter follows the course of Israel's history in chronological sequence.

He speaks, first of all, of primeval history, and then he tells of Abel, of Enoch, and of Noah, the first rounded period of human history, bringing us up to the time of Babel. Then he proceeds to tell of Israelitish history, beginning with Abraham, going on to Isaac, Jacob, and so forth, up to the time of emancipation. Patriarchal history is followed by the history of the nation, commencing with that great leader, Moses, and telling of the outgoing from Egypt and the incoming to the promised land. Then, overwhelmed with the greatness of his subject, he gives it up and says, "Time would fail me" to tell of this one, and of that one, and of the other one; who did this or who did that, who stood true, who went forward in simple reliance upon God, because his life was founded and grounded upon the belief that God was not only transcendent but imminent, that He was in all history. There follows at the close of that eleventh chapter of Hebrews one of the most eloquent passages in all the range of literature. Then he passes over into the twelfth chapter and into a new dispensation. He says, "They without us." Who are they? Who are us? They, the old dispensation. "They without us could not be made perfect." Us, the Christian dispensation. And so, passing on from age to age, from era to era, from dispensation to dispensation, we are led to see God's plan. This is not done in a haphazard or scrappy way but with exactness and in detail.

I have said that there is a great necessity for such ages, since we do not use the word *dispensation*. Yet in our homes, we do have dispensations. You do not treat your children at eighteen years of age as you treated them at eight; your method with your family is adapted to the stage they have reached, to the requirements of the case at any given time. Is it to be supposed that God has adopted any other method? Truth is graded. Revelation is progressive. God did not manifest Himself in flood tide of light to begin with—we would have been blinded and burdened—but gently, as the shining of the morning creeping over the mountain tops, and more fully the light grows until today we are living in the full noontide of it.

You can't judge the peoples of the Old Testament by the standards of the New Testament; they lived way back in the morning of the world's history. The truth, let me repeat, was graded, and God adapted His eternal and unerring ways in regard to man according to the requirements of the case and the stage at which the people had arrived at any given time.

Don't understand me to mean that God never allowed a revelation at any given time which the people could not comprehend. There is no doubt there. Search the prophets. When they told of Christ, when they told of the sufferings, the cross, and the glory that should follow, few could comprehend. Nevertheless, there have been ages, there have been dispensations, there have been periods of time in which God has been manifesting Himself and through which He has been fulfilling in history an eternal, redeeming design. That simply means that all history is a unit; underlying all history is a principle; the redeeming purpose is everywhere evident. Take the Bible and glance at it in the largeness of it. Get away from texts and paragraphs and chapters and see the thing as one great revelation in progressive unfolding.

At the beginning, you have the origin; the very word "genesis" indicates that—the start of things, the commencement, the origination. Turn right over and note the final Apocalypse; there you get not origin but issues, consummation. Things begun at the beginning are brought to their final realization at the end, and all the way between we have processes coming up out of these origins and leading into these issues. There is the start, commencement; here, continuance in the infinite providence of God leading on to that final consummation.

Human history begins in a garden and ends in a city, and that is the evidence of the progress of it. The doings of Providence are threaded together like pearls on a string. This is related to that, and that to the other. God doesn't let events fly about like autumn leaves; neither are His various dealings with man the inventions of a trying moment when driven to fresh expediency. Events dovetail into one another. Every fact is fitted and adapted to take its place in the great design of the divine Architect.

Certain it is that eternal principle underlies all human history. History may look to us like a tangled skein; we may be utterly bewildered to understand the significance of events, especially those near to us, utterly perplexed, and driven to infidelity. That is due to our frailty, our fallibility, our shortsightedness, our lack of spiritual understanding. Back of all these complex situations, these perplexing happenings, there is a divine and unerring Providence. God knows what He is going to do, and all history is a sublime unit, as we shall know some day when we see it in the length of it and in the breadth of it—the redeeming purpose having been conceived, then consummated through Jesus Christ.

What an amazing thing, therefore, is this house of history, this magnificent building that has been going up through the ages! Countless workmen have been called to work upon it—the workmen, each in his generation, passing away and others called to take their places. The building is going up, out of the wreckage and the ruin that sin has wrought, out of all the misery and suffering of fallen humanity; the building is going up, a structure designed by the Redeemer, slowly, surely. As certainly as the foundations are laid, as certainly as the building is rising from these foundations, so certainly in the fullness of time will it rise to its height, and the capstone be put in its place by divine power, and the glory shine over it—God is the builder of human history.

The Heavenly Builder

We have an external passage touching this in the sermon of Paul on Mars Hill. There he refers to the divine Builder, and he tells us that God determined the period at which each nation shall play its part in the drama of the world's history. These are the words: "He hath determined the times before appointed." He has determined their appointed seasons—that is, the appointed seasons of the nations; in other words, God has determined when the mighty peoples shall come into being, how long they shall remain in being to serve His purpose, and when they shall pass off the stage of human history.

Do you suppose it has been a matter of chance that these empires have come in the order in which they have followed one another? We think of ancient Babylon and of Assyria, of Egypt, of Chaldea, of Persia, of Greece, of Rome—try in your imagination to see this magnificent pageant of the empires through the ages. Tramp, tramp, tramp, tramp! Down the ages come these nations, these mighty powers. By chance? By accident? A mere coincidence? No! Back of all is God, the eternal, the infallible, the omnipotent, the infinitely wise, God.

God, not as a great, ruthless monster, but the God of

grace, with a redeeming heart and a redeeming purpose in His heart which He is going to fulfill in time and consummate in glory. Yes, God has determined the time at which the nations shall appear; and He has determined on principle when they shall pass away from this sphere.

If that is true of ancient history, it is just as true of modern history. We may be very perplexed at the historical configuration in our day and wonder what is going to happen. What is God's plan for the United States, for the American people, for Great Britain, for Germany, for Turkey, for Greece, for those places in the far east, and for Russia? Some are bold enough to venture upon prophecy. But whether we may discern or not discern God's present purpose and His plan for the future, this much is sure—God is on His throne. The reins on the neck of history He holds in His hand and will drive forward to its destiny. God is in charge of modern history as He was in charge of ancient history. God is in His heaven, and the believer can say all's right with the world in spite of all that is wrong. His purpose is triumphing in spite of all that seems to be wrong.

"I doubt not through the ages one increasing purpose runs." God knows what He is going to do.

And not only has He determined the time at which each nation shall rise, but the sphere it shall occupy; for the apostle goes on to say, "And the bounds of their habitation." Do you believe that the geographical configuration of the world is of accident, is of chance, is of incident? Here are seas; here are rivers; here are mountains, impassable mountains. Surely these things are indications that no nation is intended to be universal, to have all other peoples under its heel and to crush. Certain nations have had that ambition and have striven toward its fulfillment, but it has never been done. God has appointed the sphere of nations, has determined the circumstances of country, soil, climate, which shall give shape and color and life and character to those nations. What a comforting thought in these days!

In 1914 there was wild ambition on the part of one people for a place in the sun, by which was meant that all other peoples should have a place in the dust. That desire was simply a challenge to Almighty God, and that people dashed themselves up against His eternal purpose. No nation won through—or combinations won through—that great war on their own merit or because they were better than others. Every party in that conflict was guilty of sins, outstanding sins. Germany was guilty of sins; America was guilty of sins; France was guilty of sins; Great Britain was guilty of sins—all had sins. But God was in His heaven, and He was not going to depart from His divine and eternal principle even because of our sins. Right is right. The just shall live by faith. And if any nation, as any man, is found up against God and dares to challenge Almighty God, God will show Himself to be sovereign in His own universe.

Consider the order of the nations: God has arranged the nations in order. Study the map. One of the most fascinating things in the world is a map. Study the map of Palestine and that ancient world. What do you find? God chose that place for His people. That was to be the sphere of the holy seed. Now look all around it. Far away over in the east and to the south is Babylonia; up there in the north is Assyria and nearer, Syria; down in the southwest is Egypt; away over in the northwest is Asia Minor, looking toward Rome; there is the desert in the south; here are mountains in the east, and the River Jordan on the one side and the *Mediterranean* on the other side. Note that word, Mediterranean—the middle of the earth, as the word indicates. And those nations, Assyria, Babylonia, Chaldea, Egypt, crossed and re-crossed Palestine. Napoleon strutted up and down the Plain of Esdraelon and said it was the greatest battlefield in the world.

God placed His people there and arranged the nations around them; as much as man may have crumpled up the plan, God will straighten it out some day. Palestine has a part to play yet in politics, and God's covenant with Abraham is yet to be redeemed. The divine Builder has a plan, and our part is to execute it. All that vain man attempts can never thwart the purpose of God in human history.

The Builder's Methods

This leads me to the second great part in the subject, namely: the method of God in history. His activity, His action, in history is surely evident. When I was visiting Buffalo, I got into touch with a prominent man who took a special interest in history. He had specialized in this subject. At the breakfast table one morning, speaking of some matter relative to history, he interjected, in a rather uncomfortable sort of way, these words: "I don't believe in the divinity of Jesus Christ—not at all." And he passed on; there was no time to deal with the matter then. When I was leaving the hotel, I said, "My friend, you take a special interest in history. I remember your remark about Jesus Christ, and I want to say this: You can't begin to interpret history until you know by faith, resting on evidence, that Jesus Christ was more than a man, that He was the Son of God, eternally divine, in the bosom of the Father, and that He was manifested to redeem a fallen race."

All philosophies and interpretations of history that deny the full and proper deity, as well as the real humanity of Jesus Christ and His redeeming purpose for the world, are but pseudo-philosophies of history. The method of God in history is indicated on every page of holy Scripture, and the very reason for history itself is found in that purpose. If God had not intended to redeem mankind, then why did not the race perish with Adam and Eve at the gate of Eden? Why this long-drawn-out, tragic story? Why the suffering through the ages? Why the curse of the innocent, bleeding at the heels of the guilty? Why these calamities, pains, trials, if God had no redeeming purpose for mankind? You tell me that there is no such purpose, that God is not interested in us, that His creation is not a moral creation. Tell me that He has given up the race and left it to run on its own momentum, and I will say to you that I would rather not have been born, that I would far rather be a dog on the street or a bird in the tree if that is true. Because I have a conscience, a moral sense, it gives me pain when I do wrong. Why should I suffer if God has no redeeming purpose? Why should God suffer if He has no redeeming purpose? How lightly we speak and how superficially about these mighty things! It is time we stopped our puerile and infantile chatterings for a while to contemplate the majesty of God. God is in human history, working His will by a divine method. What is it? It is twofold: "We understand that the worlds were framed by the word of God"—by faith. I add, "by faith," because it is the keynote of the whole chapter. If not every verse, at least every paragraph begins with the words, "by faith." And there you get the whole secret of the divine method—by revelation on God's part, by apprehension on man's part. The revelation of God is the originating cause, and the apprehension by faith of man, the effectual cause. I want to say quite briefly and directly that whenever God has revealed Himself to man and whenever man or men have reached up and appropriated that purpose of His, God has set forward history. History is not a conglomeration of fortuitous events. History is historic; it has a plan.

Take the Bible as evidence of that. Go back to the time of Nebuchadnezzar and Daniel. Stand where they stood and see their dream and vision. What did they see? The figure of a mighty man, the head of gold, the breast and arms of silver, the belly and thigh parts of brass, the legs of iron, and the feet of iron intermingled with clay. The vision was profound, directed by the Spirit of God. We have the word that the head of gold represented the Babylonian empire. The rest is simple. The head of gold Babylonia; the breast and arms of silver must have been the nation following Babylonia, Medo-Persia. We have perfect evidence of the body to indicate that. Medo-Persia was a double nation; one arm, Media, one arm, Persia, united at the breast. The third, represented by the brass, was of course the Grecian nation, and the fourth, represented by the iron, the Roman. There is a program of history reaching up into the future for twenty-five hundred years. We can't tell what will happen tomorrow or next week. Here is a revelation telling what is going to happen twenty-five hundred years later.

Critics may bring the date of the book as far down as they please; they may deny that Daniel wrote it. It is still prophecy, and the events came to pass according to prediction. And one stage in the prediction of that book has not been reached yet: the history is not complete. There is, in this unfolded historic program, a list of four great peoples—Babylonia, Medo-Persia, Greece, Rome—and we are continuing that story in our time. There has never been a fifth empire, world-wide in dominion, as there was not a fifth metal in the image.

Take another example. God called out Abram. He said, "I will bless you and I will bless your family. I will bless the nation that shall come of you. And through you shall all the nations of the earth be blessed." There is a program of history beginning with a man and reaching an entire world. That program was made way back in the beginning of human history and came true. The proof follows. Some nineteen hundred years ago there emerged upon this scene another character—the like of which never was before and never has been since. So radical was the change which He wrought when He came, whatever interpretation you may put upon His work, that chronology has been determined by it; even the infidel and the atheist must accept Him chronologically, speaking of B.C. and A.D. The focus of all history was the incarnation of God, the appearance of God here among men. For that tremendous hour all previous history was leading up, and from it all succeeding history is flowing out. Christ is at the center of history. He is God's redeeming center; He is God's moral center; He is God's cosmic center. This whole universal system is Christo-centric.

This is the philosophy of divine revelation, and it is that which gives history its chiefest significance. Has God been fulfilling the Abrahamic covenant? Yes, in Christ—of the tribe of Judah, the Son of Jacob, the Son of Isaac, the Son of Abraham, to whom God gave the covenant. He has also fulfilled that covenant in this Book—this divine revelation—which has been given to us by Jews with perhaps one exception. The Bible came to us from the Jews; Christ was from the Jews. But the Bible is not limited to Jews, and neither is Christ limited. The Bible is the most universal book that ever has been written, and Christ is the one universal Man of all the ages. He has been revealing Himself through the successive periods of the human story. As men have apprehended the revelation, history has been set forward. We know that the future is in God's care. Think of that tremendous passage in the second chapter of Philippians: "God hath highly exalted him and given him a name which is above every name: that at the name of Jesus every knee should bow, of things in heaven, and things in earth, and things under the earth." Things celestial, things terrestrial, and things infernal shall all acknowledge Jesus, the Man of Nazareth, to be the Lord overall. That day has never yet come. We are still looking toward it. It lies in the future. Heaven will sing His praise, earth will bow to His dominion, and all hell shall cringe before Him, Who here on earth had not where to lay His head. God's purpose is to enthrone Christ. It is not the ethical Christ, not the social Christ, not the philosophical Christ that God is going to enthrone; it is the Lamb as it had been slain from before the foundation of the world. When He is enthroned in highest heaven over the entire universe, it will be the Man who died on Calvary and who bears the marks of His passion even in glory. God has a plan of history; back of all the confusion and the unbelief of men is His revelation, His many revelations, of Himself. The covenant of the Old Testament and Christ Himself, a substance of it in the New, are but the advancing stages of the divine purpose of His as it leads on to fulfillment.

Our Part

But even God can't work without man. We are called to cooperate. History is the story of the race, of the nation, of the individual; and so while God has been making His revelation, He has been making it to men and has been looking for men who will apprehend the revelation and carry forward His purpose here in time. My brethren, I point out to you that God has never wrought anything tremendous by means of masses and crowds in human history. He has wrought His wonders through the ages by individuals—people whom He could trust, people who exercise faith.

What is faith? We are told in this first verse of the chapter, "Faith is the substance of things hoped for, the evidence of things not seen." The objects, therefore, of faith are the future and the unseen; the office of faith is to give present existence to future things and vital reality to unseen things. And wherever such faith has been exercised, wherever men have laid hold of the divine revelation, God has built a new era in the human story. It is the advent of personality which alters the current of history. The sharp turning points of history are due to the rise of great personalities. It is not so much by ideas as by personalities that God sets the world forward. The mightiest civilizing powers are personalities, and the mightiest civilizing personalities are Christian men. Take Israel's religious history. It stands as a record of great names—great names, great characters, great people are the building force in their religion. On the other hand, in the religious history of Assyria, Babylonia, Egypt, and India, there is scarce one name stands out on the page. Why? Because the leaders of these peoples did not, perhaps we will have to say, could not by faith lay hold on divine revelation.

Let me lay on your minds and hearts, as I draw to a close, that it is by faith in God, self-revealed, that history has always been made. If that is true of the past, it is true of the present. Take an instance or two.

Noah—God revealed Himself to Noah concerning His purpose with reference to the wickedness of the world— the great apostasy of that time. Noah apprehended the purpose. Faith and revelation became in touch with one another, and there was no greater fool on the earth, regarded from the world's standpoint, than Noah. Think of a man building a huge ark inland with blue and unclouded skies above! Think of him preaching scores of years, warning people about a flood, mocked at, laughed at, sneered at, the butt of all the jokes, indeed—a crazy old man. But was he? He was a man who apprehended by faith the divine purpose that God was going to build a new age. The flood came; the wicked world perished; the crazy, old fool survived. God built an age upon him and set history afresh upon its course. Take the rise of Babel: God said, "Spread out." They said, "No, keep together and make a confederacy. Stay here. Build a tower reaching to heaven. Never mind God. We will please ourselves." God set the race aside and called a man. That man was from an idolatrous family and an idolatrous city, Ur of the Chaldees. He said, "Get thee out of thy country, and from thy kindred, and from thy father's house, unto a land that I will show thee." He didn't even tell him where he was to go, but He said, "I will bless you if you do this, and your family. I will give you a nation and through that nation shall all mankind be blessed." This is one of the sublimest things in all the range of Scripture. Abram went out, not knowing where he went. Another old fool, according to the standards of the world. If anyone had met Abram and asked, "Where are you going?" and Abram had replied, "I don't know," they would have said, "Fool! You don't know! How is that?" "God told me to go. He promised to show me the way. I believe God. I am going." There is no greater man in all the history of the world than Abraham. God built an age on him.

The same is true of Moses. God allowed Moses to be born and to be placed where he could study Egypt; then He sent him to the back side of the desert to study the Sinaitic peninsula. When he went back to Egypt to bring the people out, he had a thorough acquaintance with both people. He led them out to the promised land, and we talk of Mosaic dispensation today. God built an age upon him because he believed God.

Take the apostle Paul. God met with Paul as he was hastening to do the bidding of the Pharisees on the Damascus road and smote him between the stirrup and the ground. He called Paul and there followed a mighty readjustment. Paul apprehended the revelation, and God communicated a great truth to him, so that he became the chief theologian of the Church. Thirteen if not fourteen of the epistles of the New Testament came from his mind and hand because Paul believed God, and God built a dispensation upon him.

So it was with Luther. That great truth rediscovered by this man, restless in heart, uneasy in conscience, dissatisfied in mind—that truth flashed before him that justification is by faith in Christ alone. Luther studied Galatians and read a great standard commentary on Galatians and found that truth of emancipation which became the keynote of the Reformation, the watchword of the free. God built an age on Luther—the Reformation.

Down in the south of England there was a cobbler's assistant, a strange boy that people thought crazy; as he knocked nails into the boots, he studied Greek grammar. He read things that no one understood. Later he attended a council to contemplate the possibility of evangelizing the heathen. He had something to suggest: "Go forward to India," he said, "and preach the gospel to the heathen." The presiding officer silenced him. "Young man, if God wants to evangelize the heathen, He will do it without you." The young man sat down. I make bold to say that few here this morning know the name of the man who made that reply to the youth, but the name of William Carey will never be forgotten. Carey went to India, having apprehended by faith the purpose of God; the marvelous development in missionary enterprise in the last twenty-five years is the result.

And there was Morrison who went to China. The captain of the vessel on which he sailed sneeringly said, "Do you suppose you can save the Chinese?" "No," said Morrison; "I don't suppose that I can save the Chinese, but I know that God can save them." Look at the China of Morrison's day and the China of today.

Again, there is Livingstone from our own country in the north. He went forward. Folks would think him crazy too. He ventured into the jungles of Africa, tearing his way from the east to the west; home for recess and rest, then back again. What about him? A great traveler, yes. A great historian, yes. But first and last a Christian missionary, opening up a wide range in Africa for the preaching of the gospel in future days.

Our Response

So it has ever been. I want you to remember this if you forget everything else: God is building history by means of men and women whom He can trust, men and women of faith, men and women of vision, who apprehend the divine revelation and say, "Here am I, Lord, take me, equip me, send me, use me." God is still building history, but He is not building it by the men and women that are gone; He is building it by the men and the women who are here. He wants to build history by you and by me.

Where is the emphasis placed today? Not upon faith, not upon the loyal men and loyal women loyal to God, but upon armies and navies, upon power, upon commerce, upon material things. There the emphasis is being placed. We are laying stress upon our material accomplishments, upon our possessions. We are endeavoring to crush God out of His own universe; but it can't be done. Men have tried it in the past. Nebuchadnezzar aspired to world fame. He walked about upon the battlements of a great city. We learn that the walls were so thick that six chariots could drive abreast on the top of the wall. Nebuchadnezzar stood looking out over this great city, and he said, "Is not this great wonder the product of my wisdom and my power?" He was smitten in that hour with insanity and went out to eat grass in the fields like the cattle until he should understand that God was sovereign. Nebuchadnezzar aspired to world dominion, aimed at it, grasped it, lost it. God had not intended it for him. Go down a few centuries to Alexander the Great, a mighty soldier, a courageous youth. He marched away to the east, and as the story has it, he reached the far east, looked out into the infinite beyond and wept because there were not more worlds to conquer. But Alexander the Great died of profligacy in early youth. He aspired to world dominion; God had not reserved it for him, and he perished.

Lord of All, or Not Lord at All

J. Gregory Mantle, D.D. (1853–1925), an English Wesleyan circuit-riding minister, was known for both his mission work and his skills as a writer and publisher. In Deptford, England, he organized and built up a large mission known as "Central Hall" which became a model for mission work in other cities. His writing and publishing skills resulted in his publication of *The Illustrated Missionary News*, an innovative pictorial magazine. He may have been the first to use photography as an aid to missionary efforts. He carried cameras during extended tours in India, China, and Japan and came away with remarkable pictures. Mantle's magazine attracted support for numerous evangelists and Bible women (women evangelists) in India, China, and elsewhere.

Dr. Mantle spent the last twelve years of his life in the United States. He authored several books, including *The Way of the Cross*. During those years he affiliated with the Christian and Missionary Alliance, took an active part in conventions, and taught at the Missionary Training Institute in New York, now Nyack College. Taylor University in Upland, Indiana, conferred on him the honorary Doctor of Divinity degree.

This sermon is taken from *The Counterfeit Christ and Other Sermons* by J. Gregory Mantle, D.D., published in 1920 by the Christian Alliance Publishing Co., New York.

J. Gregory Mantle

5

LORD OF ALL, OR NOT LORD AT ALL

He is Lord of all (Acts 10:36).

THE QUESTION of authority has become one of the gravest questions. Never was there such a wide-spread revolt against all rightful authority as today. Even those who have been supposed to be bound together as "with bands of steel," the great trades unions, have broken away from their leaders and become "outlaws." The many want to govern, and only a few want to be governed. Whether a government be Democratic, Republican, or Autocratic, it must have some central authority. Without that central authority society cannot exist, and its overthrow inevitably leads to anarchy and chaos among the people.

All living things need a ruling force. The body is useless, and immediately plays the fool, without a head to direct its movements. An army is powerless when there is no supreme commander to issue orders. The finest vessel ever launched is certain to strike upon the rocks unless there is a captain on the bridge. There is certain to be anarchy in the family if the father forgets that he is the husband or "house-band."

If these things are true in the lower realms, how much more important is the question of authority when we speak of our relation to our Lord? A true Christian is a man or woman under the authority of the Lord Jesus Christ. His crown rights, as Lord of all, are not dependent on our recognition of them. They were the Father's gift to the Beloved Son for His great, mediatorial work: "It is in consequence of this that God has also so highly exalted Him, and has conferred on Him the Name which is supreme above every other, in order that in the Name of Jesus every knee should bow, of beings in Heaven, of those on the earth, and of those in the underworld, and

77

that every tongue should confess that Jesus Christ is Lord, to the glory of God the Father" (Phil. 2:9–11, Weymouth).

Each name of our Lord has a distinct message. The name "Jesus" is the human name, and it is a special link with the days of humiliation and sacrifice. It is a name peculiar to the Gospels, where the other names, Christ and Lord, are seldom found. "His name shall be called Jesus because He shall save His people from their sins."

At the close of the historic manifestation of Jesus, John wrote at the conclusion of his Gospel: "These things are written that ye may believe that Jesus is the Christ, the Son of God; and that believing ye might have life through His name." (John 20:31.) The word "Christ" means the Messiah, the Sent One. Christ is the Anointed One. It is His prerogative also to anoint His obedient and believing disciples with the Holy Spirit.

The name "Lord" is seldom found even in the Gospels. The Apostle John uses it because it was given to him to point men to the Son of God in all the glory of His relation to the Father, as the Lord Jesus Christ. It occurs frequently in the Acts of the Apostles, for the Church was to be built historically upon this magnificent truth: "Know assuredly" said Peter, "that God hath made that same Jesus, Whom ye have crucified, both Lord and Christ." (Acts 2:36.)

1. Lordship Means Surrender to His Sovereignty

The most perfect expression of the Lordship of Jesus in the Apostolic writings is in the letter to the Romans. The Christians at Rome and elsewhere had scruples about food. They thought the meat exposed for sale in the meat market had possibly been offered to idols. So they became vegetarians and would not touch, taste, or handle meat lest they should be defiled. Others had no such scruples but ate what was set before them, asking no questions. Others had difficulties about fast-days and feast-days.

The Apostle says: Settle these matters by making the risen Jesus Lord of your conscience. "For not one of us lives to himself, and not one dies to himself. If we live, we live to the Lord: if we die, we die to the Lord. So whether we live or die, we belong to the Lord. For this was the purpose of Christ's dying and coming to life—namely, that He might be Lord both of the dead and the living" (Rom. 14:7–9, Weymouth). No words could express more plainly than these that the purpose of Christ's death and resurrection was to win undisputed Lordship over man. "To this end"—so the passage reads in the Authorized Version—"To this end," and no other; "for this purpose," and nothing short of it, He died on the cross of Calvary. He rose from the dead and lives a life on which the tooth of time has no power in order to execute that Lordship. Therefore to dispute His sovereignty, to deny His Lordship, is to rob Him of the fruit of His passion.

Among the most honored names in the United States is that of Wendell Phillips, the incorruptible orator and statesman. He was one of the most gifted of men. He did possibly more than any other man to strike off the shackles from four million slaves. He is known to this day as "the Boston Orator" and "the man who could not be bought." Shortly before he died he was asked by a friend whether there was any crisis in his life which explained his unfaltering devotion to his Master. This was what he said: "When I was fourteen I heard Lyman Beecher preach on the Lordship of Jesus Christ. I went to my room, locked the door, and then threw myself on the floor of the room. This was what I said: 'O God, I belong to Thee; take what is Thine own; I gladly recognize Thy ownership in me; I now take Thee as my Lord and Master.' From that time to this I have never known a thing to be wrong without having an aversion to it; and I have never seen anything to be right without having an attraction to it."

Many are perfectly ready to take life from Jesus Christ who hesitate to take *law* from Him. But there can be no real loyalty unless we make Him the Lord of our conduct as well as the Savior of our soul.

How was it that Wendell Phillips was able to make that remarkable statement about aversion and attraction? Having made Jesus Lord, everything was changed. His Master stood by him in every conflict; He gave him strength for every task; He defined for him all his duties; He rejoiced in all his victories. Christ had become his Comrade, and the fully surrendered man found himself under the government of a higher will than his own for he now had a Ruler as well as a Savior.

I well remember how in my boyhood Garibaldi, the Italian Chieftain, exercised a strange fascination over me.

The freeing of Italy from the tyranny under which the people had groaned for so many years is one of the most thrilling stories in history. Garibaldi gathered round him a band of brave soldiers who never rested until Italy was free. When he had been defeated in Rome, Garibaldi issued his immortal appeal: "Soldiers, I am without money and without rewards. I have *nothing to offer* you but cold, hunger and hardship. Let him who loves his country follow me!"

This is how Mrs. Hamilton King tells the story:

> Then Garibaldi gathered all his troops
> Around him, in Saint Peter's Place, and said:
> ". . . Against the foreigner
> Shall never struggle cease in Italy
> While I can live for her. I go to bear
> Her last resistance through the provinces,
> God helping us alone. Whoever wills
> To follow me I will receive today.
> Nothing I ask from them to make them mine,
> But love for Italy, and faith in her.
> They will have neither pay nor rest with me,
> But bread and water—if we have the chance
> To find so much. I cannot promise them
> Even a grave; nothing is sure but death.
> Whoever is not satisfied with this
> Had better come no further. Every step
> Will be a step toward death, when once the gates
> Of Rome have closed behind us. Who will come?—
> Meet me at six o'clock this evening here?"
>
> These are the words that Garibaldi wrote
> Long after, remembering this day:
> "Four thousand men on foot, nine hundred horse
> Ranged themselves round me.

What wonder that with such a band of heroes Italy was freed! Garibaldi was hailed with huzzas long and loud as the savior of his country, and many felt that he should be made King. Others disputed his sovereignty though glad of his saviorship, and for a few days the brave chieftain was actually cast into prison. Then he was banished to the island of Capri, a possession which some of his grateful countrymen bestowed upon him.

Is not that exactly the way multitudes treat Jesus Christ? As their deliverer from the cruel Oppressor they gladly receive Him. But they rob Him of the fruit of His passion by refusing Him the absolute Lordship of their lives for unless He is Lord of all, He will not be Lord at all.

2. Lordship Means Surrender to His Ownership

There is a place in your heart called a throne. Someone always occupies that place. The rival claimants are Christ and Self. Which of these is on the throne? Christ will brook no rival. He will accept no divided allegiance. So long as one apartment is withheld, He will not assume control. Spirit, soul, and body belong alike to Him. There is the spirit—the citadel; there is the city—the soul; there are the walls—the body, with its five gates of access. *You* cannot keep that wonderful little kingdom for while you are watching at one gate, the crafty, sleepless enemy will come in at another. "Except the Lord keep the city, the watchman waketh but in vain."

Jesus asks for the ownership of the entire being for the whole is His by creative and redemptive right, and until all is yielded, there is discord and disharmony. Only One can bring peace to this wonderful little world. It is the Lord Jesus Christ. When we can say: "The government is on His shoulders," then every part of the little kingdom acknowledges His Kingship and rejoices in His Sovereignty. It was for this, man was created; it was for this, Jesus died and rose again.

It is exceedingly interesting to read in Bunyan's *Holy War* of the various compromises which Diabolus suggested when he found that Mansoul had to be surrendered to Emmanuel. The ambassador for Diabolus was Mr. Loth-to-Stoop, a stiff man in his way and a great doer for Diabolus. "Great Sir," said he, "that it may be known unto all men how good-natured a prince my master is, he hath sent me to tell your Lordship that he is very willing, rather than go to war, to deliver up into your hands one-half of the town of Mansoul. I am therefore, to know if your Mightiness will accept this proposition?"

Then said Emmanuel: "The whole of Mansoul is Mine by gift and purchase, wherefore I will never lose one half."

Then said Mr. Loth-to-Stoop: "Sir, my master hath said that he will be content that you shall be the nominal and titular Lord of all; if he may possess but a part."

Then answered Emmanuel: "The whole is Mine *really*, not in name and word only; wherefore I will be the sole Lord and Possessor of *all*, or of *none*, of Mansoul."

Then Mr. Loth-to-Stoop said again: "Sir, behold the condescension of my master! He says that he will be content, if he may but have assigned to him some place in Mansoul as a place to live in *privately*, and you shall be Lord of all the rest."

Then said Emmanuel: "All that the Father giveth Me shall come to Me: and of all that he hath given Me I will lose nothing—no, not a hoof nor a hair. I will not, therefore, grant him, no, not the least corner in Mansoul to dwell in: I will have it all to Myself."

A very interesting illustration of this aspect of truth is found in the life of Sir John Ramsden of Huddersfield, England. When quite a young man he saw that Huddersfield was destined from its location in Yorkshire to become a great industrial center. Property was certain to acquire a largely increased value in the near future. He therefore began quietly to purchase houses and lands. In a few years he was possessor of the whole of the town, with the exception of a cottage and garden which belonged to a Quaker gentleman.

All the overtures of the real estate men having proved futile, Sir John Ramsden himself called one day upon the Quaker to see what he could accomplish by personal influence. The usual courtesies having passed between the Knight and the Quaker, Sir John Ramsden said: "I pre-

sume you know the object of my visit." "Yes," said the
Quaker, "I have heard that you have bought the whole of
Huddersfield with the exception of this cottage and garden, and I have been earnestly solicited by your agents to
sell this. But I do not want to sell. The cottage was built
for my own convenience and suits me well. The garden,
too, is laid out to suit my tastes. Why should I sell them?"
Sir John Ramsden said: "I am prepared to make you a
very generous proposal. I will put a golden sovereign on
every inch of ground covered by this cottage and garden if
you will sell." (An English sovereign is, in normal times,
about equal both in size and value to a five-dollar gold-
piece.)

Sir John felt sure a proposal of such a nature would not
be in vain. So he inquired: "Will you sell?"

"No," said the Quaker with a mischievous twinkle in
his eye: "*Not unless you will put them on edge.*" That was
altogether out of the question, and, somewhat chagrined,
the Knight rose to leave. As he was going the Quaker
said: "Remember, Sir John, that Huddersfield belongs *to
you and to me.*"

Does anything please Satan better than to look up into
the face of Jesus and say: "That man is a prominent
officer and worker in that church, but he belongs to me
and to You"? "That woman is a diligent worker in Your
cause, but I have some stock in her life; she belongs to me
and to You." Such is the penalty of compromise, reservation, and disputed ownership.

3. Lordship Means Surrender to His Protection

The Christians to whom the Apostle Peter wrote in his
first Epistle were exposed to bitter persecution for Christ's
sake; hence the Apostle has much to say about fidelity in
suffering: "And who," he asks, "will be able to harm you, if
you show yourselves zealous for that which is good? . . .
So do not be alarmed by their threats, nor troubled; but in
your hearts consecrate Christ as Lord, being always ready
to make your defense to any one who asks from you a
reason for the hope which you cherish. (1 Peter 3:13–15,
Weymouth.)

"Care only for this," is the translation of Wiesinger, "that your hearts may be a temple of Christ, in which becoming honor may be given to Him as Lord; then will nothing further disturb you."

In other words, only make Jesus Lord and King of your life, and you have nothing to fear from devils or from men. The very end of government is the welfare of the governed. What so stirs a nation to indignation and action as an indignity done to one of its citizens? If you can put your hand on your heart and say, without compromise or reservation, "Thine is the Kingdom!" who shall harm you? "He that toucheth you," says our Sovereign Lord and Master, "toucheth the apple of mine eye."

> Enemies may seek to injure,
> Satan all his arts employ;
> God will turn what seems to harm me,
> Into everlasting joy.

The kingdom is the dominion over which the king reigns. The question is: "Who is King?" If in answer to that question you can unhesitatingly say: "Jesus is King!" then you may confidently depend upon Him to protect His kingdom.

The Scottish Covenanters, in the days of "bloody Claverhouse," as he was called because of his diabolic hatred and murderous persecution of the saints, had some wonderful experiences of the protection of Him whom they acknowledged as Lord. One day they were meeting in the shelter of a hollow in the mountain. The sentries announced to the venerable minister who was conducting the service that the dragoons of Claverhouse were upon them. It was impossible either to hide or to flee. Summoning his persecuted flock to prayer, the devoted pastor said: "O Lord, the wolf is at hand. Your defenseless sheep will be slain, apart from Your swift interposition, by those who delight in shedding their blood. Will You not, at this very moment, protect them by throwing Your cloak around them and hiding them in Your lap from the fury of the oppressor?"

In an instant the prayer was answered. A thick mist fell upon the congregation and completely hid them from the cruel Claverhouse and his dragoons, who went galloping past and saw not one of God's faithful but defenseless children.

> Fear Him ye saints, and you will then
> Have nothing else to fear;
> Make you His service your delight,
> He'll make your wants His care."

4. Lordship Means Surrender to His Enabling

"No man can say that Jesus is Lord, but by the Holy Spirit" (1 Cor. 12:3). You can say it easily with the lips, but the passage means something far deeper; it means saying it with the life. It is the Holy Spirit who alone can present and enforce the claims of Jesus to the Lordship of the life. Only He can put this blessed ideal into a sinful and divided soul. Only He can show the dishonesty of compromise and reservation. Only He can detach you from the things you once loved and spoil you forever for "the vain things that charmed you most." Only He can enthrone Jesus in the yielded heart and enable you to sanctify Christ as Lord.

His activities do not cease when Jesus has been enthroned. He will constantly discover new territory which He covets for the King. He will enable you to apply the principle of absolute surrender as you yield more and more completely to His guidance. When He says: "Will you give your Lord that voice?" You will readily respond:

> Take my voice and let me sing,
> Always only for my King.

When He says: "Will you not give your Lord His rightful share of your possessions?" You will say:

> Take my silver and my gold,
> Not a mite would I withhold.

And lest there should be anything left that is unsurrendered, you will sing:

> O come and reign, Lord Jesus;
> Rule over everything:
> And keep me always loyal,
> And true to Thee, my King.

In a soldier's order book I noticed that one-sixth of a second—just long enough for the brain to telegraph instructions to the hand or foot—was all that was allowed to prove a soldier's obedience to orders. How is it that the Great Commander has to say so often to so many: "Why call ye Me, Lord, Lord, and *do not* the things that I say?"

NOTES

The Measure of Immeasurable Power

Alexander MacLaren (1826–1910) was one of Great Britain's most famous preachers. While pastoring the Union Chapel, Manchester (1858–1903), he became known as "the prince of expository preachers." Rarely active in denominational or civic affairs, MacLaren invested his time in studying the Word in the original and sharing its truths with others in sermons that are still models of effective expository preaching. He published a number of sermon books and climaxed his ministry by publishing his monumental *Expositions of Holy Scripture*.

This message is taken from *The Best of Alexander MacLaren*, edited by Gains Glenn Atkins and published in 1949 by Harper and Brothers, New York.

Alexander MacLaren

6

THE MEASURE OF IMMEASURABLE POWER

That ye may know . . . what is the exceeding greatness of his power to usward who believe, according to the working of his mighty power, which he wrought in Christ (Ephesians 1:19–20).

"THE RICHES of the glory of the inheritance" will sometimes quench rather than stimulate hope. He can have little depth of religion who has not often felt that the transcendent glory of that promised future sharpens the doubt— "and can I ever hope to reach it?" Our paths are strewn with battlefields where we were defeated; how should we expect the victor's wreath? And so Paul does not think that he has asked all which his friends in Ephesus need when he has asked that they may know the hope and the inheritance. There is something more wanted, something more even for our knowledge of these, and that is the knowledge of the power which alone can fulfill the hope and bring the inheritance. His language swells and peals and becomes exuberant and noble with his theme. He catches fire, as it were, as he thinks about this power that works in us. It is "exceeding." Exceeding what? He does not tell us, but other words in this letter, in the other great prayer which it contains, may help us to supply the missing words. He speaks of the "love of Christ which passeth knowledge," and of God being "able to do exceedingly abundantly above all that we can ask or think." The power which is really at work in Christians today is in its nature properly transcendent and immeasurable and passes thought and desire and knowledge.

And yet it has a measure. "According to the working of the strength of the might which he wrought in Christ." Is that heaping together of synonyms, or all but synonyms, mere tautology? Surely not. Commentators tell us that they can distinguish differences of meaning between the words in that the first of them is the more active and outward and the last of them is the more inward. And so we liken them to fruit and branch and root. But we need simply say that the gathering together of words so nearly co-extensive in their meaning is witness to the effort to condense the infinite within the bounds of human tongue, to speak the unspeakable and that these reiterated expressions, like the blows of the billows that succeed one another on the beach, are hints of the force of the infinite ocean that lies behind.

And then the Apostle, when he has once come in sight of his risen Lord, as is His wont, is swept away by the ardor of his faith and the clearness of his vision and breaks from his purpose to dilate on the glories of his King. We do not need to follow him into that. I limit myself this morning to the words which I have read as my text with only such reference to the magnificent passage which succeeds as may be necessary for the exposition of this.

The Immeasurable Power

So, then, I ask you to look first at the measure and example of the immeasurable power that works in Christians.

"According to the working of the strength of the might which he wrought in Christ." The Resurrection, the Ascension, the session at the right hand of God, the rule over all creatures, and the exaltation above all things on earth or in the heavens—these are the things which the Apostle brings before us as the pattern-works, the *chef-d'oeuvre* of the power that is operating in all Christians. The present glories of the ascended Christ are glories possessed by a man; that being so, they are available as evidences and measures of the power which works in believing souls. In them we see the possibilities of humanity, the ideal for man which God had when He created and breathed His blessing upon him. It is one of ourselves who has strength enough to bear the burden of the glory, one of ourselves who can stand within the blaze of encircling and indwelling Divinity and be unconsumed. The possibilities of human nature are manifest there. If we want to know what the Divine power can make of us, let us turn to look with the eye of faith upon what it has made of Jesus Christ.

But such a thought, glorious as it is, still leaves room for doubt as to my personal attainment of such an ideal. Possibility is much, but we need solid certainty. And we find it in the truth that the bond between Christ and those who truly love and trust Him is such as that the possibility must become a reality and be consolidated into a certainty. The Vine and its branches, the members and their Head, the Christ and His church are knit together by such closeness of union as that wheresoever and whatsoever the one is, there and that must the others also be. Therefore, when doubts and fears and consciousness of my own weakness creep across me and all my hopes are dimmed, as some star in the heavens is when a light mist floats between us and it, let us turn away to Him our brother, bone of our bone and flesh of our flesh, and think that He in His calm exaltation and regal authority and infinite blessedness is not only the pattern of what humanity may be but the pledge of what His church must be. "The glory that thou gavest me I have given them."

Nor is that all. Not only a possibility and a certainty for the future are for us the measure of the power that works in us. But as this same letter teaches us, we have as Christians a present scale by which we may estimate the greatness of the power. For in the next chapter, after that glorious burst as to the dignity of His Lord which we have not the heart to call a digression, the Apostle, recurring to the theme of my text, goes on to say, "And you hath he quickened." And then, catching it up a verse or two afterward, he reiterates, clause by clause, what had been done on Jesus as having been done on us Christians. If that Divine Spirit raised Him from the dead and set Him at His own right hand in the heavenly places, it is as true that the same power has "raised us up together, and made us sit together in heavenly places in Christ Jesus." And so not only the far-off, though real and brilliant, and eye and heart-filling glories of the ascended Christ give us the measure of the power, but also the limited experience of the present Christian life, the fact of the resurrection from the true death, the death of sin, the fact of union with Jesus Christ so real and close as that they who truly experience it do live, as far as the roots of their lives are concerned, and the scope and the aim of them, "in the heavens," and "sit with him in heavenly places"—these things afford us the measure of the power that works in us.

Then, because a Man is King of kings and Lord of lords, because He who is our Life "is exalted high above all principalities and powers," and because from His throne He has quickened us from the death of sin and has drawn us so near to Himself that if we are His we truly live beside Him even while we stumble here in the darkness, we may know the exceeding greatness of His power according to the working of the strength of the might which He wrought in Christ when He raised Him from the dead.

The Unknowable Power

Secondly, notice the knowledge of the unknowable power.

We have already come across the same apparent paradox covering a deep truth in the former sections of this series of petitions. I need only remind you, in reference to this matter, that the knowledge which is here in question is not the intellectual perception of a fact as revealed in Scripture but is that knowledge to which alone the New Testament gives the noble name, being knowledge verified by inward experience and the result of one's own personal acquaintance with its object.

How do we know a power? By thrilling beneath its force. How are we to know the greatness of the power but because it comes surging and rejoicing into our aching emptiness and lifts us buoyant above our temptations and weakness? Paul was not asking for these people theological conceptions. He was asking that their spirits might be so saturated with and immersed in that great ocean of force that pours from God as that they should never, henceforth, be able to doubt the greatness of that power which works in them. The knowledge that comes from experience is the knowledge that we all ought to seek. It is not merely to be desired that we should have right and just conceptions but that we should have the vital knowledge which is and which comes from life eternal.

And that power, which thus we may all know by feeling it working upon ourselves, though it be immeasurable, has its measure; though it be in its depth and fullness unknowable and inexhaustible, may yet be really and truly known. You do not need a thunderstorm to experience the electric shock; a battery that you can carry in your pocket will do that for you. You do not need to have traversed all the length and breadth and depth and height of some newly discovered country to be sure of its existence and to have a real, though it may be a vague, conception of the magnitude of its shores.

And so, really, though boundedly, we have the knowledge of God and can rely upon it as valid, though partial; and similarly, by experience, we have such a certified acquaintance with Him and His power as needs no enlargement to be trusted and become the source of blessings untold. We may see but a strip of the sky through the narrow chinks of our prison windows, and many a grating may further intercept the view. Much dust that might be cleared away may dim the glass, but yet it is the sky that we see, and we can think of the great horizon circling round and round and of the infinite depths above there which neither eye nor thought can travel unwearied. Though all that we see be but an inch in breadth and a foot or two in height, yet we do see. We know the unknowable power that passes knowledge.

And let me remind you of how large importance this knowledge of, and constant reference to, the measureless power manifested in Christ is for us. I believe there can be no vigorous, happy Christian life without it. It is our only refuge from pessimism and despair for the world. The old psalm said, "Thou hast crowned him with glory and honor, and hast given him dominion over the works of thy hands." And hundreds of years afterward the writer of the Epistle to the Hebrews commented on it thus,

"We see not yet all things put under him." Was the old vision a dream, was it never intended to be fulfilled? Apparently so, if we take the history of the past into account, and the centuries that have passed since have done nothing to make it more probable, apart from Jesus Christ, that man will rise to the heights which the psalmist dreamed of. When we look at the exploded Utopias that fill the past; when we think of the strange and apparently fatal necessity by which evil is developed from every stage of what men call progress, and how improvement is perverted, almost as soon as effected, into another fortress of weakness and misery; when we look on the world as it is today, I know not whence a man is to draw bright hopes, or what is to deliver him from pessimism as his last word about himself and his fellows, except the "working of the strength of the might which he wrought in Christ." "We see not yet all things put under him." Be it so, "but we see Jesus," and, looking to Him, hope is possible, reasonable, and imperative.

The same knowledge is our refuge from our own consciousness of weakness. We look up, as a climber may do in some Alpine ravine upon the smooth gleaming walls of the cliff that rises above him. It is marble; it is fair; there are lovely lands on the summit, but nothing that has not wings can get there. We try but slip backward almost as much as we rise. What is to be done? Are we to sit down at the foot of the cliff, and say, "We cannot climb, let us be content with the luscious herbage and sheltered ease below?" Yes! That is what we are tempted to say. But look! a mighty hand reaches over; an arm is stretched down; the hand grasps us and lifts us and sets us there.

"No man hath ascended up into heaven save he that came down from heaven," and having returned thither, stoops thence and will lift us to Himself. I am a poor, weak creature. Yes! I am all full of sin and corruption. Yes! I am ashamed of myself every day. Yes! I am too heavy to climb and have no wings to fly and am bound here by chains manifold. Yes! But we know the exceeding greatness of the power, and we triumph in Him.

That knowledge should shame us into contrition when

we think of such force at our disposal and so poor results. That knowledge should widen our conceptions, enlarge our desires, breathe a brave confidence into our hopes, and should teach us to expect great things of God and to be intolerant of present attainments while anything remains unattained. It should stimulate our vigorous effort, for no man will long seek to be better if he is convinced that the effort is hopeless.

Learn to realize the exceeding greatness of the power that will clothe your weakness. "Lift up your eyes on high, and behold who hath created these things, for that he is strong in might, not one faileth." That is wonderful, but here is a far nobler operation of the Divine power. It is great to preserve the ancient heavens fresh and strong by His might, but it is greater to come down to my weakness, to "give power to the faint," and to "increase strength to them that have no might." And that is what He will do with us.

The Power at Work

Lastly, notice the conditions for the operations of the power. "To usward who believe," says Paul. He has been talking to these Ephesians and saying "Ye," but now, by that "us," he places himself beside them, identifies himself with them, and declares that all his gifts and strength come to him on precisely the same conditions on which theirs do to them and that he, like them, is a waiter upon that grace which God bestows on them that trust Him.

"To usward who believe." Once more we are back at the old truth which we can never make too emphatic and plain that the one condition of the weakest among us being strong with the strength of the Lord is simple trust in Him, verified, of course, by continuance and by effort. How did the water go into the Ship Canal at Eastham last week? First of all they cut a trench, and then they severed the little strip of land between the hole and the sea, and the sea did the rest. The wider and deeper the opening that we make in our natures by our simple trust in God, the fuller will be the rejoicing flood that pours into us. There is an old story about a Christian father who, having been torturing himself with theological speculations about the nature of the Trinity, fell asleep and dreamed that he was emptying the ocean with a thimble! Well, you cannot empty it with a thimble, but you can go to it with one. If you have only a thimble in your hand, you will only bring away a thimbleful. The measure of your faith is the measure of God's power given to you.

There are two measures of the immeasurable power; the one is that infinite limit of "the power which he wrought in Christ" and the other the practical limit. The working measure of our spiritual life is our faith. In plain English, we can have as much of God as we want. We do have as much as we want. And if, in touch with the power that can shatter a universe, we only get a little thrill that is scarcely perceptible ourselves and all unnoticed by others, whose fault is that? And if, coming to the fountain that laughs at drought and can fill a universe with its waters, we scarcely bear away a straitened drop or two that barely refreshes our parched lips and does nothing to stimulate the growth of the plants of holiness in our gardens, whose fault is that? The practical measure of the power is for us the measure of our belief and desire. And if we only go to Him, as I pray we all may, and continue there and ask from Him strength according to the riches that are treasured in Jesus Christ, we shall get the old answer, "According to your faith be it unto you."

NOTES

The Sole Consideration, That God Is God, Sufficient to Still All Objections to His Sovereignty

Jonathan Edwards (1703–1758) was a Congregational preacher, theologian, and philosopher, possessing one of the greatest minds ever produced on the American continent. He graduated with highest honors from Yale in 1720 and in 1726 was ordained and served as co-pastor with his grandfather, Solomon Stoddard, in Northfield, Massachusetts. When Stoddard died in 1729, Edwards became sole pastor, a position he held until doctrinal disagreements with the church led to his resignation in 1750. He played a key role in the Great Awakening (1734–44) and is perhaps best known for his sermon "Sinners in the Hands of an Angry God."

This sermon is taken from *The Works of Jonathan Edwards* (vol. 2, 1976), published by Banner of Truth Trust.

Jonathan Edwards

7

THE SOLE CONSIDERATION, THAT GOD IS GOD, SUFFICIENT TO STILL ALL OBJECTIONS TO HIS SOVEREIGNTY

Be still, and know that I am God (Psalm 46:10).

THIS PSALM seems to be a song of the church during a time of great revolutions and desolations in the world. Therefore the church glories in God as her refuge, and strength, and present help, even in times of the greatest troubles and overturnings. "God is our refuge and strength, a very present help in trouble. Therefore will we not fear, though the earth be removed, and though the mountains be carried into the midst of the sea; though the waters thereof roar and be troubled, though the mountains shake with the swelling thereof" (vv. 1–3). The church makes her boast of God not only as being her help, by defending her from the desolations and calamities in which the rest of the world were involved, but also by supplying her as a never failing river with refreshment, comfort, and joy in the times of public calamities. "There is a river, the streams whereof shall make glad the city of God, the holy place of the tabernacles of the Most High. God is in the midst of her; she shall not be moved: God shall help her, and that right early" (vv. 4–5).

In the sixth and eighth verses are set forth the terrible changes and calamities which were in the world: "The heathen raged, the kingdoms were moved: he uttered his voice, the earth melted. Come, behold the works of God, what desolations he hath made in the earth." In the verse preceding the text is elegantly set forth the manner in which God delivers the church from these calamities and especially from the desolations of war and the rage of

99

their enemies: "He maketh wars to cease unto the end of the earth; he breaketh the bow, and cutteth the spear in sunder; he burneth the chariot in the fire." He makes wars to cease when they are against His people; He breaks the bow when bent against His saints.

Then follow the words of the text: "Be still, and know that I am God." The great works of God, wherein His sovereignty appeared, had been described in the foregoing verses. In the awful desolations that He made and by delivering His people by terrible things, He showed His greatness and dominion. Herein he manifested his power and sovereignty and so commands all *to be still, and know that he is God.* For, says he, "I will be exalted among the heathen; I will be exalted in the earth."

In the words may be observed:

1. A duty described to be still before God and under the dispensations of His providence. This implies that we must be still as to *words*, not speaking against the sovereign dispensations of providence or complaining of them, not darkening counsel by words without knowledge or justifying ourselves and speaking great swelling words of vanity. We must be still as to *actions* and outward behavior so as not to oppose God in His dispensations and as to *the inward frame of our hearts*, cultivating a calm and quiet submission of soul to the sovereign pleasure of God, whatever it be.

2. We may observe the ground of this duty—*the divinity of God.* His being God is a sufficient reason why we should be still before Him, in no wise murmuring or objecting or opposing but calmly and humbly submitting to Him.

3. How we must fulfill this duty of being still before God with a sense of His divinity as seeing the ground of this duty in that we know Him to be God. Our submission is to be such as becomes rational creatures. God does not require us to submit contrary to reason but to submit as seeing the reason and ground of submission. Hence, the bare consideration *that God is God* may well be sufficient

to still all objections and opposition against the divine sovereign dispensations.

This may appear by the following things:

1. In that He is God, He is an absolutely and infinitely *perfect* being; it is impossible that He should do amiss. As He is eternal and receives not His existence from any other, He cannot be limited in His being or any attribute to any certain determinate quantity. If any thing has bounds fixed to it, there must be some cause or reason why those bounds are fixed just where they are. Whence it will follow that every limited thing must have some cause, and therefore that being which has no cause must be unlimited.

It is most evident by the works of God that His understanding and power are infinite; He that has made all things out of nothing and upholds and governs and manages all things every moment in all ages without growing weary must be of infinite power. He must also be of infinite knowledge; if He made all things and upholds and governs all things continually, it will follow that He knows and perfectly sees all things, great and small in heaven and earth, continually at one view which cannot be without infinite understanding.

Being thus infinite in understanding and power, He must also be perfectly holy for unholiness always argues some defect, some blindness. Where there is no darkness or delusion, there can be no unholiness. It is impossible that wickedness should consist with infinite light. God being infinite in power and knowledge, He must be self-sufficient and all-sufficient; therefore it is impossible that He should be under any temptation to do anything amiss for He can have no end in doing it. When any are tempted to do amiss, it is for selfish ends. But how can an all-sufficient Being who wants nothing be tempted to do evil for selfish ends? So that God is essentially holy and nothing is more impossible than that God should do amiss.

2. As He is God, He is so *great* that He is infinitely above all comprehension; therefore, it is unreasonable in

us to quarrel with His dispensations because they are mysterious. If He were a being that we could comprehend, He would not be God. It would be unreasonable to suppose any other than that there should be many things in the nature of God and in His works and government to us mysterious and which we never can fully find out.

What are we? And what do we make of ourselves when we expect that God and His ways should be upon a level with our understandings? We are infinitely unequal to any such thing as comprehending God. We may less unreasonably expect that a nutshell should contain the ocean: "Canst thou by searching find out God? canst thou find out the Almighty unto perfection? It is as high as heaven, what canst thou do? deeper than hell, what canst thou know? The measure thereof is longer than the earth, and broader than the sea" (Job 11:7–8). If we were sensible of the distance which there is between God and us, we should see the reasonableness of that interrogation of the apostle, "Who art thou, O man, that repliest against God?" (Rom. 9:20).

If we find fault with God's government, we virtually suppose ourselves fit to be God's counselors; whereas it becomes us rather, with great humility and adoration, to cry out with the apostle, "O the depth of the riches, both of the wisdom and knowledge of God! How unsearchable are his judgments, and his ways past finding out! For who hath known the mind of the Lord? or who hath been his counselor? or who hath first given to him, and it shall be recompensed unto him again? For whom be glory for ever" (Rom. 11:33–36). If little children should rise up and find fault with the supreme legislature of a nation or quarrel with the mysterious administrations of the sovereign, would it not be looked upon that they meddled with things too high for them? And what are we but babes? Our understandings are infinitely less than those of babes, in comparison with the wisdom of God. It becomes us therefore, to be sensible of it and to behave ourselves accordingly. "Lord, my heart is not haughty, nor mine eyes lofty; neither do I exercise myself in great matters, or in things too high for me. Surely I have behaved and quieted myself as a child" (Ps. 131:1–2). This consideration alone of the infinite distance between God and us, between God's understanding and ours, should be enough to still and quiet us concerning all that God does, however mysterious and unintelligible to us. Nor have we any right to expect that God should particularly explain to us the reason of His dispensations. It is fit that God should not give any account of His matters to us, worms of the dust, that we may be sensible of our distance from Him and adore and submit to Him in humble reverence.

Therefore we find that when Job was so full of difficulty about the divine dispensations, God did not answer him by particularly explaining the reasons of His mysterious providence but by showing Him what a poor worm, what a nothing he was, and how much He Himself was above him. This more became God than it would have done to enter into a particular debate with him or to unfold the mysterious difficulties. It became Job to submit to God in those things that he could not understand, and to this the reply tended to bring him. It is fit that God should dwell in thick darkness or in light to which no man can approach, which no man has seen nor can see. No wonder that a God of infinite glory shines with a brightness too strong and mighty for mortal eyes. For the angels themselves, those mighty spirits, are represented as covering their faces in this light (Isa. 4).

3. As He is God, all things are His *own*; and He has a right to dispose of them according to His own pleasure. All things in this lower world are His: "Whatsoever is under the whole heaven is mine" (Job 41:11). Yea, the whole universe is God's: "Behold the heaven, and the heaven of heavens is the Lord's; the earth also with all that therein is" (Deut. 10:14). All things are His because all things are from Him; they are wholly from Him and from Him alone. Those things which are made by men are not wholly from them. When a man builds a house, it is not wholly from him. Nothing of which the house is made has its being from him. But all creatures are wholly and entirely the fruits of God's power, and therefore, it is fit that

they should be subject to and for His pleasure. And as all things are *from* God, so they are upheld in being *by* Him and would sink into nothing in a moment if He did not uphold them (see Prov. 16:4). And all things are *to* Him. "For by him, and through him, and *to* him are all things" (Rom. 11:36). "For by him were all things created that are in heaven, and that are in earth, visible and invisible, whether they be thrones or dominions, principalities or powers: all things were created *by* him and *for* him: and he is before all things, and by him all things consist" (Col. 1:16–17). All mankind are His—their lives, and breath, and being; "for in him we live, and move, and have our being." Our souls and capacities are from Him. "All souls are mine: as the soul of the father, so also the soul of the son, is mine" (Ezek. 18:4).

4. In that He is God, He is *worthy* to be sovereign over all things. Sometimes men are the owners of more than they are worthy of. But God is not only the owner of the whole world, as all is from and dependent on Him, but such is His perfection, the excellency and dignity of His nature, that He is worthy of sovereignty over all. No man ought in the temper of his mind to be opposite to God's exercising the sovereignty of the universe as if He were not worthy of it for to be the absolute sovereign of the universe is not a glory or dignity too great for Him. All things in heaven and earth, angels and men, are nothing in comparison with Him; all are as the drop of the bucket and as the light dust of the balance.

It is therefore fit that everything should be in His hands to be disposed of according to His pleasure. His will and pleasure are of infinitely greater importance than the will of creatures. It is fit that His will should take place though contrary to the will of all other beings, and that He should make Himself His own end and order all things for Himself. God is possessed of such perfections and excellencies as to qualify Him to be the absolute sovereign of the world. Certainly it is more fit that all things be under the guidance of a perfect unerring wisdom than that they should be left to themselves to fall in confusion or be brought to pass by blind causes. Yea, it is not fit that *any* affairs within the government of God should be left without the direction of His wise providence, least of all, things of the greatest importance.

It is absurd to suppose that God is *obliged* to keep every creature from sinning and exposing himself to an adequate punishment. For if so, then it will follow that there can be no such thing as a *moral government* of God over reasonable creatures. It would be an absurdity for God to give commands for He Himself would be the party bound to see to the performance, and there could be no use of promises or threatenings. But if God may leave a creature to sin and to expose himself to punishment, then it is much fitter and better that the matter should be ordered by wisdom—who should justly lie exposed by sin to punishment and who not—than that it be left to come to pass by confused chance.

It is unworthy of the Governor of the world to leave things to chance; it belongs to Him to govern all things by wisdom. And as God has *wisdom* to qualify Him to be sovereign, so He has *power* also to enable Him to execute the determinations of wisdom. And He is essentially and invariably *holy* and *righteous* and infinitely *good*, whereby He is qualified to govern the world in the best manner. Therefore, when He acts as sovereign of the world, it is fit that we should be still and willingly submit and in no wise oppose His having the glory of His sovereignty. But we should, in a sense of His worthiness, cheerfully ascribe it to Him and say, "Thine is the kingdom and the power and the glory for ever" and say with those in Revelation 5:13, "Blessing, and honor, and glory, and power, be to him that sitteth upon the throne."

5. In that He is God, He *will* be sovereign and *will* act as such. He sits on the throne of His sovereignty, and His kingdom rules over all. He *will* be exalted in His sovereign power and dominion, as He Himself declares: "I will be exalted among the heathen, I will be exalted in the earth." He will have all men to know that He is most high over all the earth. He does according to His will in the armies of heaven and among the inhabitants of the earth,

and none can stay His hand. There is no such thing as frustrating or baffling or undermining His designs, for He is great in counsel and wonderful in working. His counsel shall stand, and He will do all His pleasure. There is no wisdom nor understanding nor counsel against the Lord. Whatsoever God does, it shall be forever; nothing shall be put to it, nor anything taken from it. He will work, and who shall let it? He is able to dash in pieces the enemy. If men join hand in hand against Him to hinder or oppose His designs, He breaks the bow; He cuts the spear in sunder; He burns the chariot in the fire. He kills, and He makes alive; He brings down and raises up just as He pleases. "That they may know from the rising of the sun, and from the west, that there is none besides me. I am the Lord, and there is none else: I form the light and create darkness; I make peace and create evil; I the Lord do all these things" (Isa. 45:6–7).

Great men and rich men and wise men cannot hinder God from doing His pleasure. He leads counselors away spoiled; He accepts not the persons of princes nor regards the rich more than the poor. There are many devices in a man's heart, but the counsel of the Lord, that shall stand, and the thoughts of His heart, to all generations. When He gives quietness, who can make trouble? When He hides His face, who can behold Him? He breaks down, and it cannot be built up again. He shuts up a man, and there can be no opening; when He purposes, who shall disannul it? And when His hand is stretched out, who shall turn it back? So there is no hindering God from being sovereign and acting as such. "He hath mercy on whom he will have mercy, and whom he will he hardeneth." He has the keys of hell and of death. He opens, and no man shuts; He shuts, and no man opens. This may show us the folly of opposing ourselves against the sovereign dispensations of God. How much more wisely they act who quietly and sweetly submit to His sovereign will.

6. In that He is God, He is able to *avenge* Himself on those who oppose His sovereignty. He is wise of heart and mighty in strength; who has hardened himself against

God and prospered? He who will contend with God must answer it. And what a poor creature is man to fight against God! Is he able to make his part good with Him? Whoever of God's enemies deal proudly, He will show that He is above them. They will be but as the chaff before the whirlwind and shall be as the fat of lambs. They shall consume into smoke; they shall consume away. "Who would set the briers and thorns against him in battle? He would go though them, he would burn them together" (Isa. 27:4).

Application

A manifold improvement might be made of this doctrine, which a little reflection may suggest to each of us. But the improvement which I shall at this time make of it shall be only in a *use of reproof* to such under convictions of sin and fears of hell as are not still but oppose the sovereignty of God in the disposals of His grace. This doctrine shows the unreasonableness and dreadful wickedness of your refusing heartily to own the sovereignty of God in this matter. It shows that you know not *that God is God*. If you knew this, you would be inwardly still and quiet; you would humbly and calmly lie in the dust before a sovereign God and would see sufficient reason for it.

In objecting and quarreling about the righteousness of God's laws and threatenings and His sovereign dispensations toward you and others, you oppose His *divinity*; you show your ignorance of His divine greatness and excellency and that you cannot bear that He should have divine honor. It is from low, mean thoughts of God that you do in your minds oppose His sovereignty, that you are not sensible how dangerous your conduct is, and what an audacious thing it is for such a creature as man to strive with his Maker.

What poor creatures are you that you should set up yourselves for judges over the Most High, that you should take it upon you to call God to an account, that you should say to the great Jehovah, what do You do?—and that you should pass sentence against Him! If you knew that He is God, you would not act in this manner. But this knowledge would be sufficient to still and calm you concerning all God's dispensations, and you would say with Eli in 1 Samuel 3:18: "It is the Lord, let him do what seemeth good in his sight." But here I shall be more particular in several things.

1. It is from mean thoughts of God that *you are not convinced* that you have by your sins deserved His eternal wrath and curse. If you had any proper sense of the infinite majesty, greatness, and holiness of God, you would see that to be cast into the lake of fire and brimstone, and there to have no rest day nor night, is not a punishment more than equal to the demerit of sin. You would not have so good a thought of yourselves; you would not be so clean and pure in your own eyes; you would see what vile, unworthy, hell-deserving creatures you are. If you had not little thoughts of God and were to consider how you have set yourselves against Him—how you have slighted Him, His commandments and threatenings, and despised His goodness and mercy, how often you have disobeyed, how obstinate you have been, how your whole lives have been filled up with sin against God—you would not wonder that God threatens to destroy you forever, but would wonder that He has not actually done it before now.

If you had not mean thoughts of God, you would not find fault with Him for not setting His love on you who never exercised any love to Him. You would not think it unjust in God not to seek your interest and eternal welfare who never would be persuaded at all to seek His glory; you would not think it unjust in Him to slight and disregard you who have so often and so long made light of God. If you had not mean thoughts of God, you never would think Him obliged to bestow eternal salvation upon you who have never been truly thankful for one mercy which you have already received of Him. What do you think of yourselves? What great ideas have you of yourselves? And what thoughts have you of God that you think He is obliged to do so much for you though you treat Him ever so ungratefully for the kindness which He has already bestowed upon you all the days of your lives? It must be from little thoughts of God that you think it unjust in Him not to regard you when you call upon Him when He has earnestly called to you, so long and so often, and you would not be persuaded to hearken to Him. What thoughts have you of God that you think He is more obliged to hear what you say to Him than you are to regard what He says to you?

It is from diminutive thoughts of God that you think He is obliged to show mercy to you when you seek it, though you have been for a long time willfully sinning against Him, provoking Him to anger, and presuming that He would show you mercy when you should seek it. What kind of thoughts have you of God that you think He is obliged, as it were, to yield Himself up to be abused by men, so that when they have done, His mercy and pardoning grace shall not be in His own power, but He must be obliged to dispense them at their call?

2. It is from little thoughts of God that *you quarrel against His justice* in the condemnation of sinners from the doctrine of original sin. It must be because you do not know Him to be God and will not allow Him to be sovereign. It is for want of a sense how much God is above you that those things in Him which are above your comprehension are such difficulties and stumbling blocks to you. It is for want of a sense how much the wisdom and understanding of God are above yours, and what poor, shortsighted, blind creatures you are in comparison with Him. If you were sensible what God is, you would see it most reasonable to expect that His ways should be far above the reason of man and that He dwells in light which no man can approach unto, which no man has seen nor can see.

If men were sensible how excellent and perfect a Being He is, they would not be so apt to be jealous of Him and to suspect Him in things which lie beyond their understandings. It would be no difficulty with them to trust God out of sight. What horrid arrogance in worms of the dust that they should think they have wisdom enough to examine and determine concerning what God does and to pass sentence on it as unjust! If you were sensible how great and glorious a being God is, it would not be such a difficulty with you to allow Him the dignity of such absolute sovereignty as that He should order as He pleases, whether every single man should stand for Himself or whether a common father should stand for all.

3. It is from mean thoughts of God that *you trust in your own righteousness* and think that God ought to respect you for it. If you knew how great a Being He is, if you saw that He is God indeed, you would see how unworthy, how miserable a present it is to be offered to such a Being. It is because you are blind and know not what a Being He is with whom you have to do that you make so much of your own righteousness. If you had your eyes open to see that He is God indeed, you would wonder how you could think to commend yourselves to so great a Being by your gifts, by such poor affections, such broken prayers, wherein is so much hypocrisy and so much selfishness.

If you had not very mean thoughts of God, you would wonder that ever you could think of purchasing a favor and love of so great a God by your services. You would see that it would be unworthy of God to bestow such a mercy upon you as peace with Him, His everlasting love, and the enjoyment of Himself for such a price as you have to offer; He would exceedingly dishonor Himself in so doing. If you saw what God is, you would exclaim as Job did, "Now mine eye seeth thee; wherefore I abhor myself, and repent in dust and ashes" (42:5–6). And as Isaiah did, "Woe is me, for I am undone, because I am a man of unclean lips; for mine eyes have seen the King, the Lord of hosts" (6:5).

4. It is from mean thoughts of God that you *contend with Him* because He bestows grace on some and not on others. Thus God does: He has mercy on whom He will have mercy; He takes one, and leaves another of those who are in like circumstances, as it is said of Jacob and Esau while they were not yet born and had done neither good nor evil (see Rom. 9:10–13). With this sinners often quarrel, but they who upon this ground quarrel with God suppose Him to be *bound* to bestow His grace on sinners. For if He be bound to none, then He may take His choice and bestow it on whom He pleases; His bestowing it on some brings no obligation on Him to bestow it on others. Has God no right to His own grace? Is it not at His own

disposal? And is God incapable of making a gift or present of it to any man? For a person cannot make a present of that which is not His own or in His own right. It is impossible to *give a debt*. But what a low thought of God does this argue! Consider what it is you would make of God. Must He be so tied up that He cannot use His own pleasure in bestowing His own gifts? Is He obliged to bestow them on one because it is His pleasure to bestow them on another? Is not God worthy to have the same right to dispose of His gifts as a man has of his money? Or is it because God is not so great and, therefore, should be more subject, more under bounds, than men? Is not God worthy to have as absolute a propriety in His goods as man has in his? At this rate, God cannot make a present of anything; He has nothing of His own to bestow. If He has a mind to show a peculiar favor to some, to lay some under special obligations, He cannot do it on the supposition because his low thoughts of God, or else they would willingly ascribe sovereignty to Him in this matter. "Is it not lawful for me to do what I will with mine own? Is thine eye evil, because I am good?" (Matt. 20:15).

God is pleased to show mercy to His enemies according to His own sovereign pleasure. And surely it is fit He should. How unreasonable is it to think that God stands bound to His enemies! Therefore consider what you do in quarreling with God and opposing His sovereignty. Consider with whom it is you contend. Let all who are sensible of their misery and afraid of the wrath of God consider these things. Those of you who have been long seeking salvation but are in great terrors through fear that God will destroy you, consider what you have heard: *be still, and know that he is God*.

When God seems to turn a deaf ear to your cries; when He seems to frown upon you; when He shows mercy to others, your equals, or those who are worse, and who have been seeking a less time than you—be still. Consider who He is that disposes and orders these things. You shall consider it; you shall know it. He will make all men to know that *he is God*. You shall either know it for your good here by submission or to your cost hereafter.

Sovereign Grace and Man's Responsibility

Charles Haddon Spurgeon (1834–1892) is undoubtedly the most famous minister of the last century. Converted in 1850, he united with the Baptists and soon began to preach in various places. He became pastor of the Baptist church in Waterbeach in 1851, and three years later he was called to the decaying Park Street Church, London. Within a short time, the work began to prosper, a new church was built and dedicated in 1861, and Spurgeon became London's most popular preacher. In 1855 he began to publish his sermons weekly, and today they make up the sixty-three volumes of *The Metropolitan Tabernacle Pulpit*. He founded a pastor's college and several orphanages.

This sermon is taken from *The New Park Street Pulpit*, volume 4, and was preached on August 1, 1858, at the Music Hall, Royal Surrey Gardens.

Charles Haddon Spurgeon

8

SOVEREIGN GRACE AND MAN'S RESPONSIBILITY

But Esaias is very bold, and saith, I was found of them that sought me not; I was made manifest unto them that asked not after me. But to Israel he saith, all day long I have stretched forth my hands unto a disobedient and gainsaying people (Romans 10:20–21).

DOUBTLESS THESE words primarily refer to the casting away of the Jews and to the choosing of the Gentiles. The Gentiles were a people who sought not after God but lived in idolatry. Nevertheless, Jehovah was pleased in these latter times to send the gospel of His grace to them, while the Jews who had long enjoyed the privileges of the Word of God, on account of their disobedience and rebellion, were cast away. I believe, however, that while this is the primary object of the words of our text, yet, as Calvin says, the truth taught in the text is a type of a universal fact. As God did choose the people who knew Him not, so has He chosen, in the abundance of His grace, to manifest His salvation to men who are out of the way. On the other hand, the men who are lost after having heard the Word are lost because of their willful sin for God does all the day long "stretch forth his hands unto a disobedient and gainsaying people."

The system of truth is not one straight line but two. No man will ever get a right view of the gospel until he knows how to look at the two lines at once. I am taught in one book to believe that what I sow I shall reap. I am taught in another place that "it is not of him that willeth nor of him that runneth, but of God that showeth mercy." I see in one place God presiding over all in providence, and yet I see, and I cannot help seeing, that man acts as he pleases and that God has left his actions to his own will in a great measure. Now, if I were to declare that

113

man was so free to act that there was no precedence of God over his actions, I should be driven very near to Atheism; if, on the other hand, I declare that God so overrules all things as that man is not free enough to be responsible, I am driven at once into Antinomianism or fatalism. That God predestines and that man is responsible are two things that few can see. They are believed to be inconsistent and contradictory; but they are not. It is just the fault of our weak judgment. Two truths cannot be contradictory to each other. If, then, I find taught in one place that everything is foreordained, *that is true*; if I find in another place that man is responsible for all his actions, *that is true*. It is my folly that leads me to imagine that two truths can ever contradict each other. These two truths, I do not believe, can ever be welded into one upon any human anvil, but one they shall be in eternity. They are two lines that are so nearly parallel that the mind that shall pursue them farthest will never discover that they converge. But they do converge and will meet somewhere in eternity close to the throne of God where all truth does spring.

Now I am about to consider the two doctrines. In the 20th verse we have taught to us *the doctrines of sovereign grace*: "But Esaias is very bold, and saith, I was found of them that sought me not; I was made manifest unto them that asked not after me." In the next verse we have *the doctrine of man's guilt in rejecting God*: "To Israel he saith, all day long I have stretched forth my hands unto a disobedient and gainsaying people."

Sovereignty in Salvation

First, then, DIVINE SOVEREIGNTY AS EXEMPLIFIED IN SALVATION. If any man be saved, he is saved by divine grace and by divine grace alone; the reason of his salvation is not to be found in him, but in God. We are not saved as the result of anything that we do or that we will, but we will and do as the result of God's good pleasure and the work of His grace in our hearts. No sinner can prevent God; that is, he cannot go before Him, cannot anticipate Him. God is always first in the matter of salvation. He is before our convictions, before our desires, before our fears, and before our hopes. All that is good or ever will be good in us is preceded by the grace of God and is the effect of a divine cause within.

Now in speaking of God's gracious acts of salvation, I notice first that they are entirely *unmerited.* You will see that the people here mentioned certainly did not merit God's grace. They found Him, but they never sought for Him; He was made manifest to them, but they never asked for Him. There never was a man saved yet who merited it. Ask all the saints of God and they will tell you that their former life was spent in the lusts of the flesh; that in the days of their ignorance, they revolted against God and turned back from His ways; that when they were invited to come to Him, they despised the invitation and, when warned, cast the warning behind their back.

They will tell you that their being drawn by God was not the result of any merit before conversion; some of them, so far from having any merit, were the very vilest of the vile. They plunged into the very kennel of sin. They were not ashamed of all the things of which it would be a shame for us to speak. They were ringleaders in crime, very princes in the ranks of the enemy. Yet sovereign grace came to them, and they were brought to know the Lord. They will tell you that it was not the result of anything good in their disposition. For although they trust that there is now something excellent implanted in them, yet in the days of their flesh they could see no one quality which was not perverted to the service of Satan.

Ask them whether they think they were chosen of God because of their courage; they will tell you no. If they had courage, it was defaced for they were courageous to do evil. Question them whether they were chosen of God because of their talent; they will tell you no. They had that talent but prostituted it to the service of Satan. Question them whether they were chosen of God because of their openness and generosity of their disposition; they will tell you that that very openness of temper and that very generosity of disposition led them to plunge deeper into the depths of sin than they otherwise would have done; they were "hail fellows, well met" with every evil man and ready to drink and join every jovial party which should come in their way.

There was in them no reason whatever why God should have mercy upon them. The wonder to them is that He did not cut them down in the midst of their sins, blot out their names from the book of life, and sweep them into the gulf where the fire burns that shall devour the wicked. But some have said that God chooses His people because He foresees that after He chooses them, they will do this, that, and the other which shall be meritorious and excellent.

Refer again to the people of God, and they will tell you that since their conversion they have had much to weep over. Although they can rejoice that God has begun the good work in them, they often tremble lest it should not be God's work at all. They will tell you that if they are abundant in faith, yet there are times when they are superabundant in unbelief; that if sometimes they are full of works of holiness, yet there are times when they weep many tears to think that those very acts of holiness were stained with sin. The Christian will tell you that he weeps over his very tears. He feels that there is filth even in the best of desires and that he has to pray to God to forgive his prayers; there is sin in the midst of his supplications, and he has to sprinkle even his best offerings with the atoning blood for he never else can bring an offering without spot or blemish.

You shall appeal to the brightest saint, to the man whose presence in the midst of society is like the presence of an angel, and he will tell you that he is still ashamed of himself. "Ah!" he will say, "you may praise me, but I cannot praise myself. You speak well of me; you applaud me. But if you knew my heart, you would see abundant reason to think of me as a poor sinner saved by grace who has nothing whereof to glory and must bow his head and confess his iniquities in the sight of God." Grace, then, is entirely unmerited.

Again, the grace of God is *sovereign*. By that word we mean that God has an absolute right to give that grace where He chooses and to withhold it when He pleases. He is not bound to give it to any man, much less to all men; if He chooses to give it to one man and not to another, His answer is, "Is thine eye evil because mine eye is good? Can I not do as I will with mine own? I will have mercy on whom I will have mercy."

A Seeking Sovereignty

Now, I want you to notice the sovereignty of Divine grace as illustrated in the text: "I was found of them that sought me not, I was made manifest to them that asked not after me." You would imagine that if God gave His grace to any, He would wait until He found them earnestly seeking Him. You would imagine that God in the highest heavens would say, "I have mercies, but I will leave men alone; when they feel their need of these mercies and seek me diligently with their whole heart, day and night, with tears and vows and supplications, then will I bless them but not before." But, beloved, God says no such thing. It is true He does bless them that cry unto Him, but He blesses them before they cry. For their cries are not their own cries, but cries which He has put into their lips; their desires are not of their own growth, but desires which He has cast like good seed into the soil of their hearts. God saves the men that do not seek Him. Oh, wonder of wonders! It is mercy indeed when God saves a seeker; but how much greater mercy when He seeks the lost Himself!

Mark the parable of Jesus Christ concerning the lost sheep. It does not run thus: "A certain man had a hundred sheep, and one of them did go astray. And he tarried at home, and lo, the sheep came back, and he received it joyfully and said to his friends, rejoice, for the sheep that I have lost is come back." No; he *went after* the sheep. It never would have come after Him; it would have wandered farther and farther away. He went after it; over hills of difficulty, down valleys of despondency He pursued its wandering feet. At last He laid hold of it. He did not drive it before Him; He did not lead it; but He carried it Himself all the way. When He brought it home He did not say, "the sheep is come back"; but, "I have *found* the sheep which was lost." Men do not seek God first; God seeks them first. If any of you are seeking Him today, it is because He has first sought you. If you are desiring Him, He desired you first. Your good desires and earnest seeking will not be the cause of your salvation but the effects of previous grace given to you.

"Well," says another, "I should have thought that although the Savior might not require an earnest seeking and sighing and groaning, and a continuous searching after Him, yet certainly He would have desired and demanded that every man, before he had grace, should ask for it." That, indeed, beloved, seems natural, and God *will* give grace to them that ask for it. But mark, the text says that He was manifested "to them that asked not for him." That is to say, before we ask, God gives us grace. The only reason why any man ever begins to pray is because God has put previous grace in his heart which leads him to pray.

I remember when I was converted to God, I was an Arminian thoroughly. I thought I had begun the good work myself, and I used sometimes to sit down and think, "Well, I sought the Lord four years before I found Him." I think I began to compliment myself upon the fact that I had perseveringly entreated of Him in the midst of much discouragement. But one day the thought struck me, "How was it you came to seek God?" In an instant the answer came from my soul, "Why, because He led me to do it. He must first have shown me my need of Him, or else I should never have sought Him. He must have shown me His preciousness, or I never should have thought Him worth seeking." And at once I saw the doctrines of grace as clear as possible.

God must begin. Nature can never rise above itself. You put water into a reservoir, and it will rise as high as that but no higher if let alone. Now, it is not in human nature to seek the Lord. Human nature is depraved, and therefore, there must be the extraordinary pressure of the Holy Spirit put upon the heart to lead us first to ask for mercy. But mark, we do not know anything about that while the Spirit is operating; we find that out afterward. We ask as much as if we were asking all of ourselves. Our business its to seek the Lord as if there were no Holy Spirit at all. But although we do not know it, there must always be a previous motion of the Spirit in our heart before there will be a motion of our heart toward Him.

No sinner can be beforehand with thee,
Thy grace is most sovereign, most rich, and most free.

Let me give you an illustration. You see that man on his horse surrounded by a body of troopers. How proud he is, and how he reins up his horse with conscious dignity. Sir, what have you got there? What are those despatches you treasure up with so much care? "Oh, sir, I have that in my hand that will vex the church of God in Damascus. I have dragged the fellows into the synagogue, both men and women. I have scourged them and compelled them to blaspheme; I have this commission from the high priest to drag them to Jerusalem that I may put them to death." Saul! Saul! have you no love for Christ? "Love to Him! No. When they stoned Stephen, I took care of the witnesses' clothes, and I rejoiced to do it. I wish I had had the crucifying of their Master for I hate them with perfect hatred, and I breathe out threatenings and slaughter against them." What do you say of this man? If he be saved, will you not grant that it must be some Divine sovereignty that converts him?

Look at poor Pilate, how much there was that was hopeful in him. He was willing to save the Master, but he feared and trembled. If we had had our choice, we should have said, "Lord, save Pilate; he does not want to kill Christ; he labors to let him escape. But slay the blood-thirsty Saul; he is the very chief of sinners." "No," says God, "I will do as I will with mine own."

The heavens open, and the brightness of glory descends—brighter than the noonday sun. Stunned with the light, he falls to the ground, and a voice is heard addressing him, "Saul, Saul, why persecutest thou me? it is hard for thee to kick against the pricks." He rises up; God appears to him: "Lo, I have made thee a chosen

vessel to bear my name among the Gentiles." Is not that
sovereignty—sovereign grace, without any previous seeking? God was found of him that sought not for Him; He
manifested Himself to one that asked Him not. Some will
say that was a miracle; but it is one that is repeated every
day in the week.

I knew a man once who had not been to the house of
God for a long time; and one Sunday morning, having
been to market to buy a pair of ducks for His Sunday
dinner, he happened to see a house of God opened as he
was passing by. "Well," he thought, "I will hear what
these fellows are up to." He went inside, and the hymn
that was being sung struck his attention. He listened to
the sermon, forgot his ducks, discovered his own character, went home, and threw himself upon his knees before
God. And, after a short time, it pleased God to give him
joy and peace in believing. That man had nothing in him
to begin with—nothing that could have led you to imagine he ever would be saved—but simply because God would
have it so, He struck the effectual blow of grace; the man
was brought to Himself. But we are, each of us who are
saved, the very people who are the best illustrations of
the matter. To this day, my wonder is that ever the Lord
should have chosen me. I cannot make it out; my only
answer to the question is, "Even so, Father, for so it seemed
good in thy sight."

I have now, I think, stated the doctrine pretty plainly.
Let me only say a few words about it. Some people are very
much afraid of this truth. They say, "It is true, I dare say,
but still you ought not to preach it before a mixed assembly; it is very well for the comfort of God's people, but it is
to be very carefully handled and not to be publicly preached
upon." Very well, sir, I leave you to settle that matter with
my Master. He gave me this great book to preach from,
and I cannot preach from anything else. If He has put
anything in it you think is not fit, go and complain to Him
and not to me. I am simply His servant; if His errand that
I am to tell is objectionable, I cannot help it. If I send my
servant to the door with a message, and he delivers it
faithfully, *he* does not deserve to be scolded. Let *me* have

the blame, not the servant. So I say, blame my Master and not me, for I do but proclaim His message. "No," says one, "it is not to be *preached.*" But it is to be preached. Every word of God is given by inspiration, and it is profitable for some good end. Does not the Bible say so? Let me tell you, the reason why many of our churches are declining is just because this doctrine has not been preached. Wherever this doctrine has been upheld, it has always been "Down with Popery." The first reformers held this doctrine and preached it. "Well," said a Church of England divine to some who railed at him, "look at your own Luther. Do you not consider him to be the teacher of the Church of England? What Calvin and the other reformers taught is to be found in his book upon the freedom of the will." Besides, we can point you to a string of ministers from the beginning even until now. Talk of apostolic succession! The man who preaches the doctrines of grace has an apostolic succession indeed. Can we not trace our pedigree through a whole line of men like Newton, and Whitefield, Owen, and Bunyan, straight away on till we come to Calvin, Luther, Zwingli; and then we can go back from them to Savonarola, to Jerome of Prague, to Huss, and then back to Augustine, the mighty preacher of Christianity; from St. Augustine to Paul is but one step.

We need not be ashamed of our pedigree; although Calvinists are now considered to be heterodox, we are and ever must be orthodox. It is the old doctrine. Go and buy any puritan book and see if you can find Arminianism in it. Search all the book stalls over and see if you can find one large folio book of olden times that has anything in it but the doctrine of the free grace of God. Let this once be brought to bear upon the minds of men and away go the doctrines of penance and confession, away goes paying for the pardon of your sin. If grace be free and sovereign in the hand of God, down goes the doctrine of priestcraft, away go buying and selling indulgences and such like things. They are swept to the four winds of heaven, and the efficacy of good works is dashed in pieces like Dagon before the ark of the Lord.

"Well," says one, "I like the doctrine; still there are very few that preach it, and those that do are very high." Very likely, but I care little what anybody calls me. It signifies very little what men call you. Suppose they call you a "hyper"—that does not make you anything wicked, does it? Suppose they call you an Antinomian—that will not make you one.

I must confess, however, that there are some men who preach this doctrine who are doing ten thousand times more harm than good because they don't preach the next doctrine I am going to proclaim, which is just as true. They have this side but not the other. They can go along with the high doctrine, but they will not preach the whole of the Word. Such men caricature the Word of God.

And just let me say here that it is the custom of a certain body of Ultra-Calvinists to call those of us who teach that it is the duty of man to repent and believe "Mongrel Calvinists." If you hear any of them say so, give them my most respectful compliments and ask them whether they ever read Calvin's works in their lives. Not that I care what Calvin said or did not say; but ask them whether they ever read his works. If they say "No," as they must say, for there are forty-eight large volumes, you can tell them that the man whom they call "a Mongrel Calvinist," though he has not read them all, has read a very good share of them and knows their spirit; he knows that he preaches substantially what Calvin preached— that every doctrine he preaches may be found in Calvin's Commentaries on some part of Scripture or other. We are TRUE Calvinists, however. Calvin is nobody to us. Jesus Christ and Him crucified and the old-fashioned Bible are our standards. Beloved, let us take God's Word as it stands. If we find high doctrine there, let it be high; if we find low doctrine, let it be low. Let us set up no other standard than the Bible affords.

Sovereignty and Responsibility

Now then for the second point. "There now," says my ultra friend, "he is going to contradict himself." No, my friend, I am not, I am only going to contradict *you*. The second point is MAN'S RESPONSIBILITY. "But to Israel he saith, All day long I have stretched forth my hands unto a disobedient and gainsaying people." Now these people whom God had cast away had been wooed, had been sought, had been entreated to be saved; but they would not. Inasmuch as they were not saved, it was the effect of their disobedience and their gainsaying. That lies clearly enough in the text. When God sent the prophets to Israel and stretched forth His hands, what was it for? What did He wish them to come to Him for? Why, to be saved.

"No," says one, "it was for temporal mercies." Not so, my friend; the verse before is concerning spiritual mercies, and so is this one, for they refer to the same thing. Now, was God sincere in His offer? God forgive the man that dares to say He was not. God is undoubtedly sincere in every act He did. He sent His prophets. He entreated the people of Israel to lay hold on spiritual things; but they would not. Though He stretched out His hands all the day long, yet they were "a disobedient and gainsaying people" and would not have His love; on their head rests their blood.

Now let me notice the wooing of God and of what sort it is. First, it was the most *affectionate* wooing in the world. Lost sinners who sit under the sound of the gospel are not lost for the want of the most affectionate invitation. God says He stretched out His hands. You know what that means. You have seen the child who is disobedient and will not come to his father. The father puts out his hands and says, "Come, my child, come; I am ready to forgive you." The tear is in his eye, and his bowels move with compassion, and he says, "Come, come." God says this is what *He* did—"*he* stretched out his hands." That is what He has done to some of you. You that are not saved today are without excuse for God stretched out His hands to you, and He said, "Come, come."

Long have you sat beneath the sound of the ministry, and it has been a faithful one, I trust, and a weeping one. Your minister has not forgotten to pray for your souls in secret or to weep over you when no eye saw him, and he has endeavored to persuade you as an ambassador from God. God is my witness, I have sometimes stood in this pulpit, and I could not have pleaded with you. In Christ's name, I have cried, "Come unto me all ye that are weary and heavy laden, and I will give you rest." I have wept over you as the Savior did and used His words on His behalf, "O Jerusalem, Jerusalem, how often would I have gathered thy children together as a hen gathereth her chickens under her wings, and ye would not." And you know that your conscience has often been touched. You have often been moved. You could not resist it. God was so kind to you. He invited you so affectionately by the Word. He dealt so gently with you by His providence. His hands were stretched out, and you could hear His voice speaking in your ears, "Come unto me, come: come, now let us reason together; though your sins be as scarlet they shall be as wool; though they be red like crimson they shall be whiter than snow."

You have heard Him cry, "Ho every one that thirsteth, come ye to the waters." You have heard Him say with all the affection of a father's heart, "Let the wicked forsake his way, and the unrighteous man his thoughts, and let him turn unto the Lord, and he will have mercy upon him, and unto our God, for he will abundantly pardon." Oh! God does plead with men that they would be saved, and this day He says to every one of you, "Repent, and be converted for the remission of your sins. Turn ye unto me. Thus saith the Lord of hosts; consider your ways." And with love divine He woos you as a father woos his child, putting out His hands and crying, "Come unto me, come unto me."

"No," says one strong-doctrine man, "God never invites all men to Himself; He invites none but certain characters." Stop, sir, that is all you know about it. Did you ever read that parable where it is said, "My oxen and my fatlings are killed, and all things are ready: come unto the marriage." And they that were bidden *would not come.* And did you never read that they all began to make excuses and that they were punished because they did not accept the invitations. Now, if the invitation is not to be made to anybody but to the man who will accept it, how can that parable be true? The fact is, the oxen and fatlings are killed; the wedding feast is ready, and the trumpet sounds, "Ho every one that thirsteth, come and eat, come and drink." Here are the provisions spread; here is an all-sufficiency. The invitation is free; it is a great invitation without limitation. "*Whosoever will*, let him come and take of the water of life freely." And that invitation is couched in tender words, "Come to me, my child, come to me." "All day long I have stretched forth my hands."

And note again, this invitation was very *frequent*. The words, "all the day long," may be translated "daily"—"Daily have I stretched forth my hands." Sinner, God has not called you once to come and then let you alone, but every day has He been at you. Every day has conscience spoken to you. Every day has providence warned you, and every Sabbath has the Word of God wooed you. Oh! how much some of you will have to account for at God's great judgment! I cannot now read your characters, but I know there are some of you who will have a terrible account at last. All the day long has God been wooing you. From the first dawn of your life, He wooed you through your mother; she used to put your little hands together and teach you to say,

> Gentle Jesus meek and mild
> Look upon a little child,
> Pity my simplicity;
> Suffer me to come to thee.

And in your boyhood God was still stretching out His hands after you. How your Sunday school teacher endeavored to bring you to the Savior! How often your youthful heart was affected; but you put all that away, and you are still untouched by it. How often did your mother speak to you, and your father warn you. You have forgotten the prayer in that bedroom when you were sick; when your mother kissed your burning forehead, knelt down and prayed to God to spare your life and then added that prayer, "Lord, save my boy's soul!" And you recollect the Bible she gave you when you first went out apprentice, and the prayer she wrote on that yellow front leaf. When she gave it, you did not perhaps know, but you may *now*; how earnestly she longed after you that you might be formed anew in Christ Jesus. How she followed you with her prayers, and how she entreated with her God for you. And you have not yet surely forgotten how many Sabbaths you have spent and how many times you have been warned. Why you have had wagon-loads of sermons wasted on you. A hundred and four sermons you have heard every year and some of you more; yet you are still just what you were.

But sinners, sermon hearing is an awful thing unless it is blessed to our souls. If God has kept on stretching out His hands every day and all the day, it will be a hard thing for you when you shall be justly condemned not only for your breaches of the law but for your willful rejection of the gospel. It is probable that God will keep on stretching out His hands to you until your hairs grow gray, still continually inviting you. And perhaps when you are nearing death He will still say, "Come unto me, come unto me." But if you still persist in hardening your heart, if still you reject Christ, I beseech you let nothing make you imagine that you shall go unpunished. Oh! I do tremble sometimes when I think of that class of ministers who tell sinners that they are not guilty if they do not seek the Savior. How they shall be found innocent at God's great day I do not know. It seems to be a fearful thing that they should be lulling poor souls into sleep by telling them it is not their duty to seek Christ and repent, but that they may do as they like about that; when they perish they will be none the more guilty for having heard the Word.

My Master did not say that. Remember how He said, "And thou, Capernaum, which art exalted unto heaven, shalt be brought down to hell: for if the mighty works, which have been done in thee, had been done in Sodom, it would have remained until this day. But I say unto you, It shall be more tolerable for the land of Sodom in the day of judgment, than for thee." Jesus did not talk thus when He spoke to Chorazin and Bethsaida; for He said, "Woe unto thee, Chorazin! woe unto thee, Bethsaida! for if the mighty works, which were done in you, had been done in Tyre and Sidon, they would have repented long ago in sackcloth and ashes. But I say unto you, It shall be more tolerable for Tyre and Sidon at the day of judgment, than for you" (Matt. 11:21–23).

It was not the way Paul preached. He did not tell sinners that there was no guilt in despising the cross. Hear the apostle's words once more: "For if the word spoken by angels was steadfast, and every transgression and disobedience received a just recompense of reward, *how shall we escape, if we neglect so great salvation,* which at the first began to be spoken by the Lord, and was confirmed unto us by them that heard him." Sinner, at the great day of God you must give an account for every warning you have ever had, for every time you have read your Bible, for every time you have neglected to read it, for every Sunday when the house of God was open and you neglected to avail yourself of the opportunity of hearing the Word, and for every time you heard it and did not improve it.

You who are careless hearers are tying faggots for your own burning forever. You that hear and straightway forget, or hear with levity, are digging for yourselves a pit into which you must be cast. Remember, no one will be responsible for your damnation but yourself at the last great day. God will not be responsible for it. "As I live saith the Lord"—and that is a great oath—"I have no pleasure in the death of him that dieth, but had rather that he should turn unto me and live." God has done much for you. He sent you His Gospel. You are not born in a heathen land. He has given you the Book of Books. He has given you an enlightened conscience. If you perish under the sound of the ministry, you perish more fearfully and terribly than if you had perished anywhere else.

Two Divine Truths

This doctrine is as much God's Word as the other. You ask me to reconcile the two. I answer, they do not want any reconcilement. I never tried to reconcile them to myself because I could never see a discrepancy. If you begin to put fifty or sixty quibbles to me, I cannot give any answer. Both are true; no two truths can be inconsistent with each other. What you have to do is to believe them both. With the first one, the saint has most to do. Let him praise the free and sovereign grace of God and bless His name. With the second, the sinner has the most to do. O sinner, humble yourself under the mighty hand of God when you think of how often He has shown His love to you by bidding you come to Himself. Yet how often you have spurned His Word and refused His mercy. How often you have turned a deaf ear to every invitation and have gone your way to rebel against a God of love and violate the commands of Him that loved you.

And now, how shall I conclude? My first exhortation shall be to Christian people. My dear friends, I beseech you do not in any way give yourselves up to any system of faith apart from the Word of God. The Bible, and the Bible alone, is the religion of Protestants. I am the successor of the great and venerated Dr. Gill whose theology is almost universally received among the stronger Calvinistic churches. But although I venerate his memory and believe his teachings, yet he is not my Rabbi. What you find in God's Word is for you to believe and to receive. Never be frightened at a doctrine; above all, never be frightened at a name. Someone said to me the other day that he thought the truth lay somewhere between the two extremes. He meant right, but I think he was wrong. I do not think the truth lies between the two extremes, but in them both. I believe the higher a man goes the better when he is preaching the matter of salvation.

The reason why a man is saved is grace, grace, grace; you may go as high as you like there. But when you come to the question as to why men are damned, then the Arminian is far more right than the Antinomian. I care not for any denomination or party, I am as high as Huntingdon upon the matter of *salvation*; but question me about damnation and you will get a very different answer. By the grace of God I ask no man's applause; I preach the Bible as I find it. Where we get wrong is where the Calvinist begins to meddle with the question of damnation and interferes with the justice of God, or when the Arminian denies the doctrine of grace.

My second exhortation is—Sinners, I beseech every one of you who are unconverted and ungodly to put away every form and fashion of excuse that the devil would have you make concerning your being unconverted. Remember, that all the teaching in the world can never excuse you for being enemies to God by wicked works. When we beseech you to be reconciled to Him, it is because we know you will never be in your proper place until you are reconciled. God has made you. Can it be right that you should disobey Him? God feeds you every day. Can it be right that you should still live in disobedience to Him? Remember, when the heavens shall be on a blaze, when Christ shall come to judge the earth in righteousness and His people with equity, there will not be an excuse that you can make which will be valid at the last great day.

If you should attempt to say, "Lord, I have never heard the word," His answer would be, "Thou didst hear it; thou heardest it plainly." "But Lord, I had an evil will." "Out of thine own mouth will I condemn thee; thou hadst that evil will, and I condemn thee for it. This is the condemnation, that light is come into the world, and men love darkness rather than light." "What hadst thou to do with that? Thou didst do according to thine own will when thou didst rebel. Thou wouldst not come unto me, and now I destroy thee forever. Thou hast broken my law—on thine own head be the guilt." If a sinner could say at the great day, "Lord, I could not be saved anyhow," his torment in hell would be mitigated by that thought. But this shall be the very edge of the sword and the very burning of the fire—"Ye knew your duty and ye did it not: ye trampled on everything that was holy; ye neglected the Savior, and how shall ye escape if ye neglect so great salvation?"

Now, with regard to myself; some of you may go away and say that I was Antinomian in the first part of the sermon and Arminian at the end. I care not. I beg of you to search the Bible for yourselves. To the law and to the testimony, if I speak not according to this Word, it is because there is no light in me. I am willing to come to that test. Have nothing to do with me where I have nothing to do with Christ. Where I separate from the truth, cast my words away. But if what I say be God's teaching, I charge you by Him that sent me, give these things your thoughts and turn unto the Lord with all your hearts.

The Providential Sovereignty of God

Paul E. Little (1928–1975) is perhaps best known for his books *How To Give Away Your Faith, Know What You Believe,* and *Know Why You Believe.* He served as Director of Evangelism for the InterVarsity Christian Fellowship and was active in evangelistic enterprises around the world, including the Lausanne Conference. He conducted evangelistic outreaches on many campuses, and he also served as associate professor of evangelism at Trinity Evangelical Divinity School, Deerfield, Illinois. His death in an automobile accident in Canada took from the church a gifted communicator and effective evangelist.

This message was given at the Moody Bible Institute "Founder's Week" conference in 1975 and is reprinted with permission from the book of "Founder's Week" messages published by the Moody Bible Institute, Chicago, Illinois.

Paul E. Little

9

THE PROVIDENTIAL
SOVEREIGNTY OF GOD

HAVE YOU ever been on the coast, either one, or anywhere, for that matter, swimming at the seashore, and found yourself knocked down by the waves, and suddenly you're in trouble? You remember how that can happen if a big wave comes and knocks you down, and you go in over your head. You begin to flail and thrash around and gasp for breath, and you're afraid. Everything is out of perspective. There isn't a great deal that matters to you at that particular point in terms of world politics or the economy, or anything else, except getting to your feet and getting your breath back again. Sometimes it happens very suddenly, unexpectedly; other times it's a gradual thing, and you're overtaken without your realizing what's happening.

You know, life is like that. Sometimes we're going along, and suddenly we're knocked down on the surf of life by some circumstance that is totally unexpected; we begin spiritually to flail around. Everything is out of focus. We're gasping for breath. We don't understand. We're panicked; a great deal doesn't matter to us that ordinarily does. Sometimes we get knocked down like that gradually, sometimes very suddenly. It may be some tragedy; it may be a physical illness that hits overnight, and none of us knows when that may happen. It may be that we flunk an exam. It may be that a relationship breaks up; it may be that we have family trouble—difficulty with children or in our marriage. It may be that our finances are in very difficult shape; what we had anticipated we could do, we couldn't do. It could be any one of a hundred things, and we flail around. It may be that some here this morning are in that situation in life at this very moment. If you're not in that situation at the moment, be thankful for it, but the time will come sooner or later when the surf of life will knock you down. The important thing is to find out how we can regain our footing and regain our spiritual breath.

The only sure footing we have in the Word of God and related to God Himself is the awareness of and the confidence of the providential sovereignty of God. It's this theme that runs through the whole of the Scripture, through the Old Testament, and into the New Testament. It is the fact that God our Creator has a loving purpose of good for each of us and that nothing happens in your life and mine by accident. I want to elaborate on this theme from the Word of God—that's the only way to get our feet back on *terra firma,* that's the only way to catch our spiritual breath with the swirling surf all around us in life. As we lay hold of that, we regain confidence and comfort and peace and joy. There is no other way. This is a theme that runs, as I say, from Genesis to Revelation. Joseph knew it. You remember the story of Joseph—literally sold down the river by his brothers. He was in all kinds of difficulty for standing for righteousness' sake and so on. He had every reason for bitterness legitimately and for all kinds of hostility. But in that classic statement in Genesis 50:20 when his brothers finally discover who he is and fear for their lives, he tells them not to worry for,

> You meant it to me for evil,
> but God meant it to me for good.

All during those years, that was the anchor that held Joseph and was the sure ground he had in the swirling surf of life.

We find it reflected in Daniel and his three friends—Shadrach, Meshack, and Abednego—in Daniel 3:17–18. You remember they were put right to the wall, literally, by Nebuchadnezzar as to whether they're going to bow down and worship. The alternative is the fiery furnace. And they say to him, "Look, we don't know what God's plan is, but we believe in His providential sovereignty." They didn't put it in those words, but that's obviously what was behind what they said. They said, "If God delivers us, fine; if He doesn't, that's fine; but in any case, we're not bowing down, so go ahead and do what you please." That's what helped them in that situation. Then there was David. David was God's anointed, but he was having a terrible time because Saul was out to kill him. David had a lot of friends who wanted to help God out. They said, "Look, there's Saul." Numbers of them said, "We'll take care of him for you; you don't even have to get your hands dirty; the blood won't be on your hands." Joab at one point said, "Look, just one throw of the spear and that's it. We'll take care of the whole thing." He no doubt gave very plausible reasons to David, since he had already been anointed, why this might be appropriate. But David, knowing God's providence and His care and His love, said in 1 Samuel 26:11:

> God forbid that I should touch the Lord's anointed.

David didn't try to do God's work for Him, even though there was a lot about it that must have been swirling surf.

The Principle at Work

I'd like to think with you about how this principle operated in Paul's life and see something of its implications for us personally. The beauty and the power and the strength of the Word of God is that these things are written for our example upon whom the end of the ages have come, and all of these things can minister strength and grace and power and love to us. That's why the Bible is a living Book and applicable at every time in history and in every culture and in every situation. The passage and incident from which I'd like us to think this thing through is Philippians 1:12–26, realizing that Paul here is writing from an imprisonment. He's not writing from the local Holiday Inn but is chained to a Roman soldier on a rotating basis. You think you've got problems with your roommate; imagine if he or she was chained to you, and you couldn't get away, and there was a rotation. Imagine what that would do to you, not just after two days, but after two weeks, two months. This is the situation Paul is writing from. Realize that as we read these verses.

I want you to know, brethren, that what has happened to me has really served to advance the gospel, so that it's become known throughout the whole praetorian guard, and to all the rest that my imprisonment is for Christ. And most of the brethren have been made confident in the Lord because of my imprisonment, and are much more bold to speak the Word of God without fear. Some indeed preach Christ from envy and rivalry, but others from good will; the latter do it out of love, knowing that I am put here for the defense of the gospel. The former proclaim Christ out of partisanship, not sincerely, but thinking to afflict me in my imprisonment. What then? Only that in every way, whether in pretense or in truth, Christ is proclaimed, and in this I rejoice, yes, and I will rejoice. For I know that through your prayers and the help of the spirit of Jesus Christ, this will turn out for my deliverance, as it is my eager expectation and hope that I shall not be at all ashamed, but that with full courage, now as always, Christ will be honored in my body, whether by life or by death. For to me to live is Christ, and to die is gain. If it is to be life in the flesh, that means fruitful labor for me, yet which I shall choose I cannot tell. I'm hard pressed between the two. My desire is to depart and be with Christ, for that is far better; but to remain in the flesh is more necessary on your account. Convinced of this, I know that I shall remain and continue with you all for your progress and joy in the faith, so that in me you may have ample cause to glory in Christ Jesus because of my coming to you again.

Paul was amazing. He was able in that situation to see the providential, loving sovereignty of God in his past, in his present, and in his future, which was completely unknown. Imagine all that had gone into that statement, that amazing statement in verse 12:

I want you to know, brethren, that what has happened to me has really served to advance the gospel.

You remember everything that had preceded this? This whole incident really began when Paul was falsely accused in Jerusalem in Acts 21:29. He was sent to jail on what we today would call a bum rap. He was accused by the Jews of taking a Gentile into the temple because they had seen Trophimus the Ephesian with him. That was not the case, but nevertheless there was such an uproar he was put into what we call today protective custody. He was then held for two years. We've got problems today in our prisons with people who are unable to make bail, who languish in Cook County Jail here and in other prisons across the country for months and months and months without coming to trial, even though they may ultimately be declared innocent. That was Paul's problem for two years. He was kept also by two people, one of whom thought he was going to get some money, Felix, according to Acts 24:26. That's not an unknown problem in our time, either. And the other one who took over, Festus, according to Acts 24:27, held him for political reasons because he wanted to appease the Jews.

Paul, unjustly put in prison in the first place and then held wrongly for financial and political reasons, ultimately appeals to Caesar because they decide they're going to send him back from Caesarea, where they'd send him for protective custody, to Jerusalem. He knew that was a hanging jury, so he said, "Nothing doing, I'm a Roman citizen." He appealed to Caesar. Then on the way he's almost shipwrecked. Read Acts 27 and all that was involved in that. Nobody would listen to him; the ship almost went down; they finally got with it and listened to him. God gave him a vision:

> I believe God, that it shall be even as it was told me.

Then he comes to Rome, and here he is in jail, originally probably in prison, later in his own lodgings but chained on a rotating basis, awaiting trial under an uncertain, corrupt Emperor Nero. Certainly doesn't give you a great deal of confidence in the system when you think about Nero and all that went on under that whole set up. It's out of that context that Paul says:

> I want you to know, brethren, that what has happened to me has really served to advance the gospel.

Paul saw the hand of God in his path, and he saw that nothing had happened to him by accident and that God had a purpose in it.

I wonder if you have recognized that fact about your past. Everyone of us has things in our past that we wonder about, things in our past that we think if we had been doing it, we might do differently. But it's God who has brought us through the past, and we need to recognize that. God is the One who put you in the family you're in. He's the One who gave you the abilities you have and the disabilities you have. He is the One who has allowed struggles of various kinds to come into your life, be they family or marriage, with roommates or with friends, financial, academic, or physical. He has been the One who has allowed this, and He's been at work uniquely in your life. Have you ever thanked God for His providential, sovereign, loving care in your life and all that has gone into it up to this point? This is what kept Paul going and kept him from being overwhelmed in the surf of life.

Or are you by any chance consumed with second-guessing—"If only I had said this, or done that, or somebody hadn't done this, or done that, the whole thing might have been different." Do you ever drive yourself wild with second-guessing in life? It's a futile experience, and one that as Christians we needn't go through and shouldn't go through because it indicates a lack of trust. Are you fighting against your background? Do you wish you were somebody other than you are? Or do you wish you were doing something other than what you're doing? You may find yourself fighting against God if you fail to realize as Paul did here that the whole of your past has had the hand of God in it, and it's useless to be worried about the past. God is concerned about the present and our relationship to Him from here on in, even with failure in the past. You didn't take God by surprise when that happened. God loves you and me, and He has a purpose for good in all of the providential, sovereign working of His will in all of the details of our lives that have brought us to this very moment. Paul, despite everything that could have made him bitter and frustrated, says in the light of that astonishing background:

I want you to know, brethren, that what has happened to me has really served to advance the gospel.

Now I want us to see very clearly that accepting the providential sovereignty of God as a basic principle of life in which we can rejoice and be thankful does not mean that we are totally passive. It does not mean acceptance of what the Muslims call *kismet*, the blind, inexorable outworking of fate. It does not mean that we have no freedom, but it does mean that our God is a loving Father and that He works in our lives for good. We are to be active where that is required, but we are to accept that which we cannot control as coming from the hand of God.

Notice that Paul was very active, even though obviously this principle had worked itself into the marrow of his bones, and that's why he was able to respond and write like this from Rome. Paul acted where he could. You remember when he was thrown into prison in Philippi, again falsely accused. Paul and Silas sang at midnight; the jailer was converted; and they had a great time! When the magistrates discovered he was a Roman citizen, they were really shaken. They said, "Oh, we're very sorry; we made a bad mistake. Please pardon us. Feel free to slip out of town; good-bye." If you read Acts 16:37 and following, you find that Paul says, "Nothing doing. You violated my rights as a Roman citizen. You come down here personally and get us out of jail and escort us out of town."

Paul wanted it clear to them and everybody else in the Roman Empire that it was not against the law to preach the gospel. Paul didn't just say, "Oh, well, okay, we'll just sort of accept that; we'll sneak out of town, and maybe we can get out before dawn," and so forth. He made a scene, if you like, for the glory of God. He accepted the fact that he was in jail. He and Silas sang, somebody was converted, and there was great blessing. But he was very active because he knew what the law was and that it had been violated, and he always had in mind the furtherance of the gospel. Likewise in Acts 25 when they wanted to send him down to a hanging jury from Caesarea to Jerusalem, Paul knew that was not right; so he exercised his right and appealed to Caesar. He didn't just say, "Well, whatever happens, I take as God's will." He wasn't totally passive. There were things over which he had some control and for which he took responsibility. I want us to be very clear that realizing this tremendous truth of the providential sovereignty of God doesn't mean that we are passive in life. Likewise when you read the account of the shipwreck in Acts 27, Paul didn't just say, "Well, I wonder how it's all going to turn out; let's just sort of see how things are." He practically took command of the ship. He gave instructions as to what to do and how to operate, and they survived. He acted when he could to change the situation; but when he couldn't change things, he accepted them.

The Principle Applied

Now that's exactly, I think, the principle that should apply to us in our lives. There may be things in your life right now that you're expecting God to do that He's never promised to do. He wants you to move and change them. There may be temptations you're facing, and you think, "Well, I wonder why God allows this? Lord, get me out of them." And the Lord may be saying to you, "Look, you're the one who walked right into the jaws of the temptation. You're the one who's responsible with the strength that I give you to avoid them." 1 Corinthians 10:13 says:

> No temptation has taken us but such as is common to man; but God is faithful, who will with the temptation always provide the way of escape. And he'll not allow us to be tempted above what we are able.

But that's the kind of temptations that take us unawares. Some of us walk into relationships, walk into situations which we know are going to send us down the tubes, and then we say, "God, why don't you do something?" God has never promised to do that, and we are to be active in overcoming then.

Some of us are seeking guidance. I hope you're seeking it actively, not just saying, "Well, Lord, I'm waiting for the writing on the ceiling." Get all the information you can about all kinds of things. Tell the Lord every day that you're prepared to do and go anywhere and do anything that He wants you to do but get all the information you can. It's information and contact and this kind of thing that God often uses as He brings to your mind the principles of the Word of God and relates them to the information that you have. Don't just be totally passive and wait for some kind of "liver shiver" that will be some divine spiritual Morse code that will give you guidance in the situations of life. God will lead and direct, but He expects you to be active.

The whole question of a job, finances, interpersonal relationships—"Lord, O please, why can't You solve the problems we've got in our marriage, with our children, or between people that I know?" God may be saying to you, "Look, I'm working in your life. I've allowed these things to happen for a purpose; it hasn't happened by accident, but I expect you to do something." You're the one who should take the initiative and ask forgiveness. You're the one who should forgive unilaterally, if necessary, if you've been wronged, even apart from the other person, and through you He will minister love and grace and power.

It may be that God wants us to take action in some area of life to get us out of the surf, in addition to realizing that nothing has happened in our lives by accident. Paul saw the tremendous truth of the loving, providential sovereignty of God in the whole of his life in the past at the time he's writing. But that did not cause him to be passive about the situations of life in which he had some responsibility and was able to do something. The same can be true of us. Thank God for your past, if you never have and realize that all of it has come from the hand of God with the purpose of love.

But then Paul saw the providential sovereignty of God in his present situation as well, when he says in verse 13:

> The way that this thing has really advanced the gospel is that it has become known throughout the whole praetorian guard and to all the rest that my imprisonment is for Christ; and most of the brethren have been made confident in the Lord because of my imprisonment, and are much more bold to speak the word of God without fear.

Paul was amazing. He never missed opportunities. He didn't throw up his hands and say, "Well, what can I do in this kind of situation? I've got a very limited audience." He realized that God had a purpose in this. You can almost picture the situation as various guards would come and literally get plugged into Paul, chained to him. After a period of time Paul would get talking with them and say, "Now, by the way, are you interested in spiritual things?" And they obviously would get the message. Undoubtedly, many came to Paul with great curiosity because they had heard who he was. The thing that was amazing about this man was that he wasn't in jail for insurrection or for stealing or for murder—he was there for religious reasons. This was an amazing thing to them, and no doubt his case was notorious.

People apparently were allowed to come and visit Paul. He no doubt talked to them and taught them the Scripture, and the guards were listening to this whole thing. And often, you know, there's a bank shot that way. You may not be able to speak to somebody directly. But in the third person you can often see flapping ears; people are drinking up everything you're saying, even though you're directing it to another person. No doubt all of that was part of Paul's approach and ministry here.

The fact of the matter was that through this crack Roman legion of ten thousand people, the Word of God spread. Paul says it's not only the praetorian guard but all the rest. Tradition has it that this praetorian guard was a crack unit and was shifted throughout the whole Roman Empire; the gospel was first brought to Great Britain through men who were converted in this praetorian guard, possibly through the life and witness of Paul. He said the second thing is that:

> The brethren have gained confidence in the Lord because of my imprisonment.

It's amazing. Rather than being an occasion for giving up the ghost because they were looking for the great Apostle Paul to come and do all the work, Paul's example was a real encouragement to the believers in the way he was praising God for all of His providential, sovereign care. Also, these brethren came to the realization that their trust had to be in God rather than in Paul. Whenever you have special meetings in your church or you go into any kind of Christian activity like that, where is your trust and confidence? Is it inherently in the people involved whom you invite, no doubt after great prayer? Or is your confidence ultimately in God Himself that He will do something? If it's in people, you'll be in difficulty if it's not possible for the one to whom you were looking to be there. You'll be disappointed very often because people in whom you have confidence sometimes don't come through. But if your confidence is in God, you won't be disappointed even though there may be all kinds of changes in a situation.

One of the great comforts to me personally, both in running conferences and also when I am invited to speak at a conference, is that God, if He has to, will speak through Balaam's donkey. I often feel, I must say, very much like Balaam's equestrian friend when I stand up to speak, but I'm trusting God that over and beyond that He will speak in power. These brethren gained confidence, and this was in the present.

Do you see in your own life that God can and will do something through you uniquely, if you're willing to make yourself available to Him? Or do you think primarily in terms of your being a set up for other people whom God will work through? Now very often we're in a situation—I've been in it many times—in which we're arranging things for others to come through whom God will minister. But God will also work through you personally in situations if you will allow Him to do it. Paul saw the working of God in his present situation. He saw that the Word of God, the gospel, had become known to the whole praetorian guard with all of the implications of that; he saw and was encouraged by the way the brethren took confidence in the Lord rather than in him and actively communicated the gospel.

Have you recognized the providential sovereignty of God in your immediate circumstances? Maybe you're going through something right now that is really bothering you, and you don't understand it. You don't see quite how it all fits together. You are heading down one road, and there are blocks on that road. God seems to be doing and saying something else. Take courage and heart; ask God to show you what He's doing in your life in the immediate present. Maybe there are dimensions of blessing that you have overlooked. But even if you can't see them as clearly as Paul saw them here, realize in the light of the whole of the Word of God and in the face of Jesus Christ that He is working in your present situation. And if you are willing to allow Him to do it, He will work in and through you.

How God Works

Now let me make a couple of observations as to why Paul was used of God even in prison or when he was restricted like this. We may get a clue as to how, though our situation and circumstances may be quite adverse at the moment, God may nevertheless work in and through our lives for a blessing. In the first place, Paul wasn't wallowing in self-pity. He wasn't saying, "Why me?" You know, Paul would have had all kinds of possibilities. Here's the great apostle, the man who had a great public ministry, and God allows him to get stuck in a situation where he's attached to one other person and allows this to go on month after month after month. You can imagine Paul thinking in that situation, "Lord, you know, I had such a great ministry going. I had such visions for public meetings here in Rome, and I want to get over to Spain. Lord, look at this, look at this guy who's plugged into me here. Talk about a ball and chain, how can I possibly have any kind of a significant ministry in this kind of situation?" Paul didn't wallow in self-pity and say, "Why me? Why couldn't it have been somebody else?" He took it as from God and made the best of it.

In the second place, Paul didn't think God had forgotten him. You ever think that? Maybe you're going through that now and wondering, "Boy, I wonder if the Lord really knows my situation and my problem." It's that feeling that God has deserted us that can really bother us in a present situation. Paul didn't feel that. He knew that God knew all about him; as a matter of fact, he took his current situation as the appointment of God. In verse 16 he says:

> They know [and they must have gotten it from him] that I am put here for the defense of the gospel.

Paul says, "Not only did it not happen by accident, but it's part of Your design that I am put here for the defense of the gospel." He was not at all feeling that God had forgotten him. Do you feel God has forgotten you? Remind yourself this morning as our Lord says in Matthew 10 that the very hairs of your head are numbered. He knows all about that decision you've got to make in a couple of days. He knows the agony of heart through which you're going, if that's your situation. He knows all about it, and He hasn't made a mistake. He's set you in a situation for a particular purpose.

The third reason that Paul was used of God is that he was part of the now generation. You know, we hear a lot about the now generation. Well Paul in verse 20 says:

> It is my eager expectation and hope that I shall not be at all ashamed, but that with full courage now as always Christ will be honored in my body.

Paul could have said, "Well, Lord, I guess this prison experience is going to be an interlude in my ministry, and I can sort of coast here and forget the whole thing." By no means. Paul realized that God's will, as I've said on other occasions, is not some package out in the future that we blindly grope after, having felt it was let down out of heaven on a string. It is more like a scroll that unrolls every day. God had a will and a plan and a purpose for Paul today and tomorrow and the next day and the day after that. God has a plan and purpose for you today. The only day that you and I have to live for Jesus Christ is today.

I hope particularly that you who are students will not say, "I'm sort of putting that projection off until I get out. I'm going to live the Christian life, have a quiet time, be nice to my family and friends, and so forth and so on. But right now I'm just caught in the rat race of survival and getting through." Don't kid yourself. The Christian life is not some great successful exploit out in the future. It's merely the succession of an accumulation of successful days of living for Jesus Christ. And it's only what you and I put into today for Jesus Christ that will determine the quality content of our Christian lives. It's not some great amorphous blob out in the future. Paul was part of the now generation. He didn't wallow in self-pity. He didn't say, "God, you must've forgotten me." He realized God had a purpose for him, even in the midst of his difficulties, for blessing; he wanted to see that will worked out in his life. How about you and me today, even though we may be in the middle of the surf?

Paul was amazingly preserved from bitterness, even when there were those who preached the gospel, as he says,

> From envy and rivalry, but others from good will. The latter do it out of love, knowing that I am put here for the defense of the gospel; the former proclaim Christ out of partisanship, not sincerely, but thinking to afflict me in my imprisonment. What then? Only that in every way, whether in pretense or in truth, Christ is proclaimed, and in that I rejoice.

Paul was an amazingly magnanimous man. In my own judgment this doesn't refer here to the Judaizing teachers because their teaching was false. Apparently there were people who preached the gospel, even though their motives were impure, and maybe they did it in a little different way from what Paul did. But Paul was thankful that the gospel was preached—that was his only concern. He wasn't concerned about his evangelistic association or his personal reputation. Even though no doubt many of these people did this in an attempt to increase Paul's frustration, Paul was glad that the gospel was preached. That's an attitude of magnanimity you and I need to get hold of.

You know, we're great at criticizing other people sometimes, kind of a reverse of this principle. I often think of D. L. Moody's statement when people complained about the way somebody was doing something they would do differently if they were doing it. D. L. Moody would reply, "Well, I like the way I'm doing something better than the way you're doing nothing." There's a great deal of truth in that. If and when people criticize you down the road for the way you do it—the music is too fast or too slow—you know, there are all kinds of things that can get people shook up—fleas on elephants that they're great at picking out—be comforted by that and don't be disturbed. If people go off and do it a different way, recognize Paul's attitude here and don't allow yourself to be overwhelmed by jealousy or concern or bitterness in that realm either. Paul saw the power of God in his present.

Finally, Paul saw the providential sovereignty of God in his future. Paul's future was uncertain. Nero was totally unpredictable. Paul didn't know what was going to happen to him. He had a kind of a hunch, a conviction, that he was going to come through this situation, and in fact he did. But he says:

> I know that whatever happens, through your prayers and the help of the Spirit of Jesus Christ, this will turn out for my deliverance.

He wasn't at that point talking about being freed from jail, but for his good. And then he says he's in a great tension because he wants now as always to have Christ honored in his body, whether by life or by death. He says:

> To me to live is Christ, to die is gain.

And then he goes on to say:

> If it's life in the flesh, that's further fruitful labor for me; and if it's death, that's fine. I'm in the presence of Christ.

Paul incidentally wasn't looking to death as a cop-out, but rather as the fulfillment of the ministry that God had given him. Paul had confidence in God for the future. It was totally uncertain, but Paul was obviously at peace.

Now your future and mine are uncertain. Many of you don't know where you're going to be and what God wants you to do. Many of you don't know how you're going to get the money to finish school perhaps. Some of us have difficulties and problems we don't know the outcome of, and we're concerned about it. But if we've seen the providential sovereignty of God at work in our past, and we are aware of His presence and power in the immediate present, then we can relax so far as the future is concerned. We can thank God that though we don't know what the future holds, we can rest secure knowing that the same God of love who gave Himself in Jesus Christ to die for us has got a purpose of blessing and good for us in the future. What about the future that haunts you today? There has never been more uncertainty in the world at large about the future than now. There are no safe places in the world politically, physically, and economically. Yet our lives are in God's hands; we can, with confidence, trust Him to unfold it as we are active in working out His purposes in our lives.

God grant then that each of us will be able to thank God for all that has gone into our past, including those things that may have really given us bitterness and second thoughts. But He'll give us the vision to see His presence and power and providence at work in our immediate situation. As we have butterflies about the unknown future, we can relax and trust God who has demonstrated His love for us that what He does in the future and what He allows will be according to His loving will. Nothing in the future, as it hasn't in the past or in the present, will happen by accident. We can rest with confidence in that.

NOTES

Prayer to the Most High

Alexander Whyte (1836–1921) was known as "the last of the Puritans," and certainly his sermons had the Puritans' preciseness as he magnified the glory of God and exposed the sinfulness of sin. He succeeded the noted Robert S. Candlish as pastor of Free St. George's and reigned from that influential Edinburgh pulpit for nearly forty years. He loved to "dig again in the old wells" and share with his people truths learned from the devotional masters of the past. His evening Bible courses attracted the young people and led many into a deeper walk with God.

This sermon is taken from *Lord, Teach Us to Pray,* published by Hodder and Stoughton.

Alexander Whyte

10

PRAYER TO THE MOST HIGH

Lord, teach us to pray (Luke 11:1).
They return, but not to the Most High (Hosea 7:16).

THE MOST HIGH. The High and Lofty One, That inhabits eternity, whose Name is Holy. The King Eternal, Immortal, Invisible, the Only Wise God. The Blessed and Only Potentate, the King of kings, and Lord of lords. Who only has immortality, dwelling in the light which no man can approach unto. Who no man has seen, nor can see. Great and marvelous are Your works, Lord God Almighty. Just and true are Your ways, You King of saints. Who shall not fear You, O Lord, and glorify Your Name? For You only art Holy. God is a Spirit: Infinite, Eternal, and Unchangeable in His Being. Wisdom, Power, Holiness, Justice, Goodness and Truth—lo! these are parts of His ways; but how little a portion is heard of Him! But the thunder of His power who can understand? The Most High!

Now the greatness of God is the true index and measure of the greatness of man. God made man in His own image. God made man for Himself and not for any end short of Himself. "Man's chief end is to glorify God and to enjoy Him forever." "In Thy presence is fullness of joy: at Thy right hand there are pleasures forevermore." "Then will I go unto the altar of God, unto God my exceeding joy." "Enter thou into the joy of thy Lord." The higher, then, that God is, the higher is our everlasting destination to be. The more blessed God is, the more blessed are we purposed and predestinated to be. The more surpassing all imagination of prophets and psalmists and apostles the divine nature is—the more true it is that eye has not seen, nor ear heard, nor has it entered into the heart of man what God has prepared for them who are forever to be made partakers of the divine nature. "I in them, and Thou in Me. And the

149

glory which Thou gavest Me, I have given them: that the Love wherewith Thou hast loved Me may be in them: and I in them."

And then, in order to hedge up and secure all these to their everlasting exaltation and blessedness, God has made it the supreme law of all His laws to us that all men shall, above all things else, seek their own chief end. And He has made it the sin of sins, the one unpardonable sin in any man, to come short of his chief end—which is the full enjoying of God to all eternity. And the prophet Hosea has all that in his mind and in his heart, when he utters that great evangelical invitation and encouragement, "Come and let us return unto the Lord." And he has all that in his mind and in his heart also when he utters the sore lamentation and bitter accusation of the text, "They return, but not to the Most High."

Prayer As Our First Step

Now it is necessary to know, and ever to keep in mind, that prayer is the all-comprehending name that is given to every step in our return to God. True prayer—the richest and the ripest prayer, the most acceptable and the most prevailing prayer—embraces many elements: it is made up of many operations of the mind and many motions of the heart. To begin to come to ourselves—however far off we may then discover ourselves to be—to begin to think about ourselves is already to begin to pray. To begin to feel fear or shame or remorse or a desire after better things is to begin to pray. To say within ourselves, "I will arise and go to my Father"—that is to begin to pray. To see what we are and to desire to turn from what we are—that also is to pray.

In short, every such thought about ourselves and about God and about sin and its wages and about salvation, its price and its preciousness; every foreboding thought about death and judgment and heaven and hell; every reflection about the blood and righteousness of Jesus Christ and every wish of our hearts that we were more like Jesus Christ; all our reading of the Word, all our meditation, reflection, contemplation, prostration and adoration; all faith, all hope, all love; all that, and all of that same kind—it all comes, with the most perfect truth and propriety, under the all-embracing name of "prayer"; it all enters into the all-absorbing life of prayer.

> Prayer is the soul's sincere desire,
> Uttered or unexpressed:
> The motion of a hidden fire
> That trembles in the breast.
>
> Prayer is the burden of a sigh,
> The falling of a tear,
> The upward glancing of an eye
> When none but God is near.
>
> Prayer is the simplest form of speech
> That infant lips can try:
> Prayer the sublimest strains that reach
> The Majesty on High.

How noble then is prayer! How incomparably noble! Who would not be a man of prayer? What wise, what sane man will continue to neglect prayer? "Ask, and it shall be given you; that your joy may be full."

Now, be it understood that neither this text nor this sermon is addressed to those who do not pray. Both the prophet and the preacher have their eye this morning on those who not only pray, on occasion, but who also are at pains to perform all those other exercises of mind and heart that enter into prayer. They read the Word of God; they meditate on what they read; they sing God's praise at home and in the sanctuary; and they repent and reform their lives. What more would this prophet have than that? My brethren, this is what he would have: he would have all that done to God. The prophets are all full of this very same accusation and remonstrance and protest that all the acts prescribed by the law of God were done; but, not being done to God, the most scrupulous, the most punctual, the most expensive service was no service at all in God's sight and estimation. "To what purpose is the multitude of your sacrifices unto Me? saith the Lord. When ye come to appear before Me, who hath required this at

your hands, to tread My courts? Bring no more vain obla-
tions: incense is an abomination unto Me: the new moons
and Sabbaths I cannot away with: it is iniquity, even the
solemn meeting. Your new moons and your appointed
feasts My soul hateth. They are a trouble unto Me: I am
weary to bear them." That is the climax, indeed, of all
such accusations and indignations; but all the prophets
are full of the same accusation. It is all summed up in the
short and sharp accusation of the text, "They return, but
not to the Most High."

But then on the other hand, we are very happy in having the other side of this matter most impressively and
most instructively set before us in a multitude of most
precious psalms. And it is this indeed that makes the Psalms
the mother and the model of all subsequent books of true
devotion: we see in them those true and spiritual worshipers in Israel returning, and returning to the Most High.
Take one of those truly returning psalmists, and hear him
and imitate him.

> Against Thee, Thee only, have I sinned, and done this evil in
> Thy sight. Wash me thoroughly from mine iniquity, and
> cleanse me from my sin. Behold, Thou desirest truth in the
> inward parts: and in the hidden part Thou shalt make me to
> know wisdom. Hide Thy face from my sins: and blot out all
> mine iniquities. Create in me a clean heart, O God: and
> renew a right spirit within me. Cast me not away from Thy
> presence: and take not Thy Holy Spirit from me. The sacrifices
> of God are a broken spirit: a broken and a contrite heart, O
> God, Thou wilt not despise" (Ps. 51:2, 4, 6, 9–10, 17)

That, my brethren, is true returning to God. And God
meets all such returnings and says, "Come now and let us
reason together: though your sins be as scarlet, they shall
be as white as snow: though they be red like crimson,
they shall be as wool.

Now, while we have all that in the Old Testament for
our direction, for our imitation, and for our encouragement, we, New Testament people, are met at every step
of our return to God with this great utterance of our
Lord on this whole matter: "No man cometh unto the
Father but by Me." And, no sooner have we heard that—

no sooner do we believe that—than every step of our return to the Most High from that day takes on a new direction. All our religious exercises, public and private, are now directed toward Him of whom the apostle says, "He dwelt among us, and we have heard, we have seen with our eyes, we have looked upon, and our hands have handled, of the word of life. That which we have seen and heard declare we unto you, that ye also may have fellowship with us." Fellowship, that is, in their fellowship with the Word made flesh, till he that has seen and heard the Son, has as good as seen and heard the Father; and till all our prayers and praises are to be directed, in the first place, to the Word made flesh, even as in the Old Testament they were directed immediately and only to the Most High.

Prayer and Christ's Presence

But, with all our New Testament nearness to God; with the Most High, now and forever, in our own nature; with Jesus Christ, the one Mediator between God and man, near to every one of us—are we any better of all that? When we return in prayer and in praise, do we return into the very presence of Jesus Christ? Or are we, with all that, as far from Him as the formalists in Israel were far from the Most High? Have we taken any real assistance and any true advantage out of the Incarnation in this matter of prayer? The Incarnation of the Son of God has brought many assistances and many advantages to the children of men. And one of the greatest and most momentous is this—that the Most High is now so near us and especially so near us when we pray.

Now, is that so? As a matter of experience and practice is that so to us? Do we practice the presence of Christ when we pray? Do we think ourselves and imagine ourselves into His presence when we stand up to sing and kneel down to pray? Have we as keen and as quick and as intense and as ever-present a sense of His presence as we have of the presence of our fellow-worshipers? When, at any time, we kneel in secret, is it no longer secret as it once was; but is the whole place now peopled with the presence of Christ? And, in public worship, are we so overshadowed and overawed with His presence that all those fellow worshipers around us are, for the time, but so many mere shadows to us? Is it so? Is it becoming so? It will assuredly be so when we return to Jesus Christ in our prayers and when He presents us and our returning prayers to the Most High.

Speaking for myself, I have found this device very helpful in my own returnings to my Savior. And I recommend this same device to you. Make great use of the Four Gospels in your efforts to return to Jesus Christ. Think that you are living in Jerusalem. Think that you are one of the Twelve. Think that you are one of those amazing people who had Him in their streets and in their homes every day. And fall down before Him as they did. Speak to Him as they did. Show Him your palsies and your leprosies as they did. Follow Him about, telling Him about your sons and daughters as they did. Tell Him that you have a child nigh unto death as they did. Wash His feet with your tears and wipe them with the hair of your head as they did. Work your way through the four Gospels from end to end; and, all the time, with a great exercise of faith, believe that He is as much with you as He was with Simon the leper, with the Syro-Phoenician woman, with Mary Magdalene, with Lazarus who had been four days dead, and with the thief on the cross. Read and believe and pray. Fall at His feet. Look up in His face. Put Him in remembrance. Put your finger on the very place and ask Him if that is really true. Ask Him if He did and said that. Ask Him if you are really to believe that and are safe in your case, also, to act upon that.

If you are a scholar, say to yourself as the old scholarly believers said—*Deus ubique est et totus ubique est*; set out again to return to God in Christ in the strength of that. And, if you are unlearned like Peter and John, well, like them say: "Were not these His words to us while He was yet with us—Lo, I am with you alway, even to the end of the world." And act your faith again as if it was indeed so. And the more pure and simple and absolute faith you put in Him and into your prayer—the more will He take plea-

sure in you till He will say to you: "O woman! Woman! I
have not found so great faith, no, not in all Israel. Be it
unto thee and unto thy daughter, even as thou wilt!" "I
came to this at last," says a great Scottish saint: "I came at
last to this, that I would not rise and go away till I felt sure
I had had an audience. And I sometimes felt as sure that I
was having an audience as if He had been before me in the
body."

But, before he came to that, he often said—and the
saying has become classical in the North of Scotland—
lamenting his parched heart he often said, "Surely I
have laid my pipe far short of the fountain." And so he
had. And so have we. No words could describe our case
better than the text and that other saying so like the
text, for we also are always returning, but not to the
Most High. We are always laying our pipe, but not up to
the fountain. We are always engaged in the exercises of
public and private religion. We are not atheists. We are
not scoffers. We do not forsake the assembling of ourselves together. We are glad when it is said to us—Let
us go up to the House of the Lord. We enter into His
courts with thanksgiving and into His gates with praise.
At the time appointed, we partake of the Lord's Supper;
and, again, we bring our children to be baptized. We
make our vow, and we pay it. And when at any time we
fall into a besetting sin, we hasten to repent and to
reform our lives. We incline our hearts again to keep
God's commandments.

But, with all that, this so heart-searching, this so soul-
exacting text discovers us and condemns us. We return to
all that; but we do not return to the Most High. We lay our
pipe up to divine ordinances—to the most spiritual of divine ordinances: up to prayer and to praise and to meditation and to Sabbaths and to sacraments. But, all the time,
all these things are but so many cisterns. All these things,
taken together, are not the Fountain. God is the Fountain.
And when we return to God when we lay our pipe up to the
true Fountain of living waters—then we taste an immedi-
ateness of communion, an inwardness of consolation, a
strength of assurance, a solidity of peace, and a fullness of

joy that are known to those only who truly return to the Most High. Until we are able to say—and that not out of a great psalm only but much more out of a great personal and indisputable experience—"Whom have I in heaven but Thee? and there is none upon earth that I desire beside Thee. My flesh and my heart faileth: but God is the strength of my heart, and my portion forever."